TWENTY THINGS FOR GRANDPARENTS OF INTERFAITH GRANDCHILDREN TO DO (AND NOT DO)

TO NURTURE JEWISH IDENTITY IN THEIR GRANDCHILDREN

RABBI KERRY M. OLITZKY AND PAUL GOLIN

Torah Aura Productions

Torah Aura Productions • 4423 Fruitland Avenue, Los Angeles, CA 90058
(800) BE-Torah • (800) 238-6724 • (323) 585-7312 • fax (323) 585-0327
E-MAIL <misrad@torahaura.com> • Visit the Torah Aura website at www.torahaura.com

Twenty Things for Grandparents of Interfaith Grandchildren to Do (and Not Do) to Nurture Jewish Identity in Their Grandchildren

ISBN 1-891662-89-9 • 9781891662881 •Copyright © 2007 Torah Aura Productions

MANUFACTURED IN UNITED STATES OF AMERICA

TABLE OF CONTENTS

IN THEIR HOME AND IN THEIR LIVES

ACKNOWLEDGMENTS

This book would not have been possible without the helpful suggestions of many people, as well as those who opened up their hearts and their families to us so that we might all learn. In particular, we thank Dr. Maurice Elias, Andréa Hanssen, Sarah Littman Olitzky. In addition, we thank our colleagues at the Jewish Outreach Institute who work tirelessly to help shape an inclusive, welcoming Jewish community, one that opens hearts, homes, and doors for those who have intermarried. Without their professional competence, friendship and support, much of what we do at the Jewish Outreach Institute would be impossible. We also thank our families for providing us with the unconditional support to do what may be among the most challenging but is certainly the most rewarding work to be done in the Jewish community.

Rabbi Kerry M. Olitzky and Paul Golin

$\mathcal{I}$NTRODUCTION

Because this book reflects the challenges facing many grandparents with regard to the Jewish identity of their grandchildren, this was not an easy book to prepare. Neither will it be an easy book to read, nor will it be simple to implement some of the suggestions in its pages. However, if you want to help nurture the Jewish identity of your grandchildren—in a home where one of their parents is not Jewish—we recommend carefully considering each recommendation. While there are no guarantees, we want you to be in the best possible position to make a difference in their lives. Research conducted by the Jewish Outreach Institute continues to indicate the often-overlooked importance of the role that grandparents play—even long distance—in the development of the religious identity of a child.

Often bubbling under the surface of relationships in families where children have intermarried are unspoken tension and emotions. They may surface during specific periods of time, whether they be holiday visits, vacations, or life-cycle events. These feelings have to be reckoned with, especially because what is suggested in this book will assuredly have an impact on them.

With a supportive non-Jewish son- or daughter-in-law, many of these suggestions can be seamlessly implemented. Your child and his/her partner may welcome your participation in the religious upbringing of the child, especially if the parents have made a clear choice to raise a Jewish child. However, many so-called interfaith families (so-called because they may not be practicing any faith at all) have not made a decision to raise children in one particular religion and therefore will be no more welcoming of your participation than that of the children's other grandparents, who are presumably not Jewish. In such cases, as well as those in which your grandchildren may be being actively raised in another religion entirely, you will have to deal carefully with some of the recommendations in this book, since they may appear to be clandestine, and you will want to be sensitive to your grandchild's other grandparents, who may be experiencing some of the same doubt and anxiety you are feeling.

If you take away one message from this book and all of its helpful suggestions, it is this: **NEVER GIVE UP.** Religious identity is not something that is fixed in time. It takes a circuitous route throughout one's life. (Consider the Jewish path that you have traveled.) And regardless of how children are raised, they eventually make their own decisions about religion, religious practice, and how they one day will raise their own children.

1. ℬE THE BEST JEW *YOU* CAN BE.

We have all heard it before: "Do as I *say*, not as I *do*." It seems like the first thing that comes to mind when parents have no good answer when their children ask, "If *you* don't do it, why should I?" Even very young children have a keen sense of role modeling, of learning what's important to members of their family by just observing their actions. If you're currently not "doing" anything Jewish, don't despair. You can still be (or become) a great Jewish role model for your grandkids. You wouldn't have picked up this book unless being Jewish has meaning to you. Discovering what is meaningful for you and then acting on it for yourself is the best way to help your grandchildren find meaning in Judaism for themselves.

Start simple. This is the best advice we can offer you. While your first inclination may be to try to sway others with regard to their actions, the emphasis needs to be on what *you* can do, not what others can or will do. And the best influence that any of us can have on others is leading by our own example. Since Jewish tradition has always favored behaviors over anything that we might say or even believe, it is not surprising that our emphasis is on doing rather than saying. While our *words* may have some influence over our adult children and

3

our grandchildren, our *actions* speak much more loudly—and honestly—especially to our grandchildren.

Some people may think that it is too late to do anything and fret over all the things that they "coulda, shoulda" done while they had the opportunity, when their children were still under their direct influence. But regrets will not help us; the past is only valuable insofar as what we can learn from it. As one friend likes to say, "This is crooked thinking." So let's start thinking straight. It is never too late to engage in a meaningful experience, especially a meaningful Jewish experience, because there is such an array of possible activities. This is not to say that starting a serious involvement in Jewish life when you haven't had one in many years (or perhaps your entire life) should be taken lightly. As the Rabbis in the Talmud teach us, "All beginnings are difficult." But perhaps it is the act of actually *beginning* that is the difficult part. Because the most important thing is not what you do specifically to start an engaged Jewish life, but that you start.

On the other hand, if you have been involved Jewishly for a long time, take a good, hard look at what you've been doing and the way you've been doing it. Consider how others read the decisions you have made, because this may be the way that your grandchildren will read your actions, too.

Totally distraught, one friend came to us after his son decided to marry someone who was raised as a Mormon. His son told him that it didn't matter, because the family didn't do anything Jewish when he was a child. He knew his son was right. So he determined to use his son's future wedding as an impetus to take up Jewish practice. He said to us, "I apparently was not much of a model for my children. At least I can start now to be one for my grandchildren." As we helped guide him in his Jewish journey, what was originally motivated by his grandchildren turned meaningful for himself as he discovered a depth of meaning and connection he hadn't been expecting. Unexpectedly, the motivation for increased Jewish activity—that he thought was coming from the outside—came from inside himself. And this motivated him to practice even more.

People learn the importance of things from the role models provided them by those they love and respect. This is particularly critical for young children, whose moral and subsequent religious compass is shaped by observing and learning from those in positions of authority, those who are held in high esteem, and especially those whom they love. So what is it that you want to share with your grandchildren? Well, start with an inventory for yourself of what you find meaningful in Judaism, then do it, and by doing it you'll be sharing it. There are simple things to begin with. The Jewish calendar is filled with holidays, most of which can serve as possible entry points. For young children, there are the fun holidays: Hanukkah, Purim, Passover. Carry on your own family traditions or, where none exist, create them! If you can cook, recruit the kids to help you (i.e., learn from you). If you can sew, create Purim costumes. If your connection is through the history of the Jewish people, find fun books and innovative ways to share that history.

Holidays are an easy entry point, but they are only one entry point. Some people find that the intellectual challenge of study is a way into Judaism. When we repeatedly engage a sacred text, we can claim the right to really call it our own. This is especially true for those who navigate a religious life through the lens of the intellect. And it is especially helpful for working with your older grandchildren, especially for those who demonstrate a pronounced intellectual curiosity. Others are looking for a spiritual tie to Jewish tradition. Thus the text becomes an environment in which we can learn more about God and in so doing learn more about ourselves. For us, spirituality is about closing the gap that exists between the individual and God. Sometimes rituals—when they are effective—help to bring us closer to God as well. But effective rituals do not just happen. While they should not be contrived, they do have to be planned—and repeated.

The idea of modeling for others is also important as our grandchildren grow older. It is not something that is reserved for early childhood. While we, of course, need to make our holiday observances fun, interesting and accessible to young children, it is important that such an approach not eclipse the later opportunity to participate as adults. What we do should emphasize that holidays and ritual observances are important to us as adults; we are not merely doing things for our grandchildren when they are children. If Judaism is reserved only for childhood—even if we are successful in providing them with wonderful childhood experiences—then Judaism may eventually be left behind along with the remnants of childhood as our grandchildren move into adolescence and beyond.

For example, some Passover rituals repeated year after year provide comfortable, familiar rhythms we look forward to and enjoy. But if you find the family seder bogging down in monotonous readings, what can you do to liven things up? Well, when was the last time you challenged your family by changing the haggadah you read from? Or selecting different sections to read? Some families like to "build" their haggadah in loose-leaf binders so that they can continue to add and delete from year to year. As they come across something relevant, they add it to the binders in preparation for using it at Passover. Children who have helped in selecting things to include look forward to their use during the holiday. It becomes "their" contribution to the accumulating seder experience. As with all Jewish holidays, there is an almost infinite depth in meaning to explore, and the Passover story is perhaps the deepest of all. Digging deeper in the weeks before the holiday can arm you with some interesting insights to share. You can dig into Jewish history or into your own family history. Perhaps there are funny stories from your own childhood seders that you can share. Taking the time to prepare before the holidays can provide lasting memories for your kids and grandkids.

Remember: Jewish identity is nurtured through the creation of Jewish memories, one layer at a time. For us, that is really what effective Jewish education is all about. These memories, created one after another, nurture the roots of identity as we grow older and as we carry them into adulthood. These are the important memories needed to help shape the religious decisions of your grandchildren. Do what you can to make sure that these memories are significant and plentiful. And don't stop. As soon as you have finished with one, it is time to start the next one.

We can hear you now: "I don't have the skills to do what they are asking." Start with the basics. The easiest, most uncluttered experiences often provide us with the most significant memories. Focus on one thing that you want to do. Don't worry about it being perfect. And don't idealize it in your planning. You don't want to be in a position of thinking that one glitch in your planning spoiled the whole thing. Sometimes the unplanned parts of an experience shape the memorable aspects of it for children. Then weeks later, and then months later, whenever appropriate, remind the grandchildren of the experience. This serves to bolster the memory. As an example, try creating your own filling for Purim hamantaschen. Experiment with unusual ingredients. That way you can create a secret recipe together.

One word of caution: Don't limit your relationship or the things that you do together to things related to Jewish rituals or holiday experiences. Play baseball or go to the zoo together. Work together on homework, or even just sit and watch a favorite movie. Jewish identity is built in the context of a relationship, and the relationship must be as holistic as possible. But remember: The building of a Jewish identity is not the shortest line between two points. It has its many bumps along the way. Never give up. Jewish identity is the circuitous journey that one travels on throughout life. If you make sure your own Jewish journey is rich and fulfilling, it will inevitably influence the loved ones in your life, including your grandchildren.

2. ASSESS THE SITUATION WISELY.

One of our favorite Yiddish expressions reads something like this: "To the unlearned, old age is winter. To the learned, it is harvest time." Some people read this folk saying as an impetus for acquiring cultural literacy while young, an affirmation of the need to pursue learning throughout one's lifetime. But we think that the ancestors who shaped this statement had something more in mind. The phrase really speaks about the potential wisdom that can emerge directly from the experiences of living. After all, that is the definition of wisdom—the things that you *learn* from living *your* life. Wisdom does not come from divine revelation, nor does it come from knowledge that others give you. Wisdom, and our response to it, arises from our direct and personal engagement with life.

When approaching your intermarried adult children about the Jewish identity of your grandchildren, it's time to "harvest" your life's wisdom. You may hear lots of outside opinions, but it's more important for *you* to know where your adult children stand with regard to the Jewish status and education of your grandchildren than to follow what your peers might have to say. Don't make any assumptions. Consider only what you see or have been told explicitly by your kids. Before taking any action, wisely assess the situation. In order to do so, it seems to us that it will be necessary to determine into which category of interfaith children your grandchildren fit. Determining their category will help you to decide on an appropriate action plan. Like most things, these categories can be further subdivided and are extremely nuanced. This is what makes a course of action difficult to navigate. But don't fret; it can be navigated, and you are able to do so.

Of grandchildren born to intermarried parents, the first category is those who are being raised as Jews. At the Jewish Outreach Institute we actually refer to this category simply as "Jewish families", since that is the religion of the family, irrespective of the faith of origin of the non-Jewish adult partner. While you will always have to be sensitive to the kids' other grandparents, the decision to raise Jewish children generally allows for an easier relationship with your grandchildren. Of course, we also have to consider the impact that results from which grandparents live closer to their grandchildren.

The second group of kids—and their parents—can best be described as practicing what we like to call "American civil religion"—frequently enhanced by a mix of Jewish and Christian holidays such as Hanukkah and Christmas, Easter and Passover. With the exception perhaps of the isolated segments of Christian holiday celebration—even when they occur in secular forms—these families look like the majority of American Jewish families, those whose adult partners were both born as Jews. In other words, regardless of the family makeup, American Jews tend to acknowledge American secular holidays through their celebration more extensively than they do Jewish holidays. While this group of interfaith grandchildren presents us a diverse array of challenges, we still have significant potential for success (read: future Jewish continuity) with them.

The third group of kids is being raised as Christians or some mix of Judaism and Christianity (we'll call them "Christian-leaning families" for the purposes of this book). This group will be the most difficult and, as a result, potentially cause you the most emotional distress. But it doesn't mean that it will be impossible to reach them. It also doesn't mean that the decision that they have made today will carry them through the rest of their lives. And it certainly doesn't mean that they will not acknowledge in some way their Jewish family heritage. It is in this last notion—that has been borne out by our documented research—that you will have to concentrate: Nurture whatever latent spark of Judaism you can find and in the form that you find it.

The aforementioned three models are just that: models. They can't be used to perfectly describe the unique individuals that comprise your adult child's family. For example, in the "Jewish family" model where one parent is from another background, there may still be the trappings of that other background. It admittedly took us a while to come to terms with the notion that sometimes a Christmas tree is just a tree! The fact (many might say the *sad* fact) is that some Jewish households, even where there is no intermarriage, put up trees during the holidays and see this practice as a seasonal/secular act rather than a religious one. But if the kids are going to Hebrew school, if they are celebrating the Jewish holidays and identify themselves as Jews, the mere sight of a Christmas tree does not bounce them automatically into the "Christian-leaning" model. To do so may be an overreaction with unfortunate consequences.

Sam grew up in a Jewish family, although his mother wasn't Jewish. While they acknowledged the Christian holidays celebrated by his mother's relatives, it never occurred to him that he was anything but Jewish. It wasn't until he entered college that he even considered his mother's background relevant to his Jewish identity, but some of the kids at school questioned it. Wendy, on the other hand, was raised in a family that celebrated a smattering of Jewish and Christian holidays. She recalls that Thanksgiving and Fourth of July were always more important to her family than any of the religious holidays, regardless of their origin. Her parents told her, "You can choose your own religion when you grow up. We wanted to expose you to both." Wendy confided in us that she was really exposed to neither and really didn't know when the time would come that she "grew up" and could make such a choice. Peter, however, was raised by a practicing Christian mother and sent to religious school at the local church. Nevertheless, he always felt a connection to the Jewish people. After all, half of his family is still Jewish.

In all three cases, look for the cues that the families left for us to find. The answers to some of these questions will be helpful: What decisions, if any, were made before marriage and then before the birth of children? What promises were made to relatives, particularly other grandparents, about how the children would be raised? Promises to dying relatives are particularly important. They give us insight (and a measure of guilt, to be sure). Have your adult children joined a synagogue or church? Have they enrolled your grandchildren in any religion-based educational program (school, camp, etc.)? Of whom is their social group comprised? What kind of Jewish experiences did your children have when they were younger? Have they had any negative experiences with Jewish institutions related to their interfaith marriage?

And now come some even more difficult questions: How is your general relationship with your adult children? Are there other things that are important to you—that you hold dear—that they have rejected? Make sure that the issues related to interfaith marriage are not providing camouflage for these relationship issues.

Now that you have begun to assess the situation, what do you do? Remember that the assessment has to be ongoing. Events occur daily that have the potential to impact on the decisions we have taken, the choices we have made. This is what provides the foundation for the other sections of the book.

3. $\mathcal{S}$TAY OPTIMISTIC ABOUT THE INHERENT POTENTIAL FOR CLAIMING JEWISH IDENTITY.

Consider the experiences of the ancient Israelites in Egypt. From the most difficult of circumstances—the dark days of slavery in Egypt—God redeemed the Jewish people. Our ancestors left behind four hundred years of slavery in order to taste the sweet freedom of the desert. Early on their way, they encountered God before continuing their journey to their ultimate destination: a Land of Promise. Passover, which narrates the exodus experience, is all about hope and optimism. It is no coincidence that this holiday is celebrated in the spring, when we generally feel most optimistic about the future. For those of you who live in northern climes that boast cold, unrelenting winters, you know that there is nothing more inspiring than the regeneration of nature each year in the spring. Buds burst into bloom. The dormant plants that we thought were dead suddenly come to life. This is an expression of nature's own unyielding optimism, its own version of faith in the future.

Just as our ancestors experienced many highs and lows during their delivery from Egypt, you may become disillusioned in the quest to influence the Jewish identity of grandchildren. We must keep sight of the fact that this is a journey, a long trek with many exciting events and possibilities—and obstacles—along the way. Positive transformation won't happen overnight. But with persistence, patience, and optimism, we *can* help foster Judaism within our intermarried children's households.

Often what frustrates us most is the apathy of our own adult children toward their Jewish identity. Perhaps they feel alienated from the Jewish community. Or maybe they had an experience that made them question their relationship to Judaism. Given the experience that many interfaith couples have had with the organized Jewish community, it is not surprising that they may still be angry. This anger frequently translates into apathy or, worse, hostility toward anything Jewish. Unfortunately, such animus is easily read by their children.

If we are honest with ourselves, we may have to admit to inadvertently contributing to their feelings of estrangement. It might have resulted from reacting emotionally—without fully thinking through the lasting sting of our reactions—when they told us that they had fallen in love with someone who wasn't Jewish and were planning to get married. To add to the difficulty, we may be fearful that our desire for grandchildren who affirm their Jewish identity will get in the way of our relationship with our adult children, the parents of our grandchildren. The navigation of a relationship with our children and grandchildren will probably be something that we have to be careful about for the rest of our lives.

No matter what came before, there is almost always still an opportunity to fan into flames the nascent spark of Jewish identity that resides inside the young souls of your grandchildren—if we are able to discern it. It may be challenging to do so, and there will certainly be risks along the way. In the best of circumstances, the road to Jewish identity has its twists and turns. Nevertheless, we can promise you that it is possible for your grandchildren to eventually embrace a Jewish identity when currently there appears to be none, or even when (just to make matters more difficult) it appears that there is no parental support for our efforts. We never know when these children will decide to claim their Jewish identity, nor what will be the specific turning point. They may reach the fullness of their Jewish identity long after your ability to influence them directly wanes.

For example, we are witnessing an amazing phenomenon on college campuses today. Children of intermarriage are identifying themselves as Jews, even when their parents claimed not to have raised them Jewishly. These college kids are now taking courses in Jewish studies in record numbers, and for many it's their first time to really learn about their heritage, an incredibly powerful experience that transcends academia. Nobody can fully explain this anomaly yet, but our hunch is that it has to do with *pride*. The level of pride among Jews in America is very high, and that pride is contagious. Perhaps the children of intermarriage whose parents were indifferent about religion nevertheless absorbed Jewish pride from other sources: cultural icons like movie star comedian Adam Sandler; friends who are being raised Jewish; and yes, even their proud Jewish grandparents. We'll talk about showing your Jewish pride in the next chapter, but the point here is that the positive status associated with being Jewish in North America today is one very good reason for you to remain optimistic about your grandchildren eventually wanting to explore their

Judaism. The most important thing for you, the grandparents, to remember: Don't give up; even amid the most trying of circumstances; stay optimistic about the future.

In your optimism about the future—and a present that is brimming with possibility—you are actually teaching others about the essential gift of the Jewish people to humanity. This is the gift of optimism and hope. Because this gift has been shared with so many others, it is comforting to know that you are not striving alone, even if at times it might feel that way. Perhaps no one else in your family is motivated to support you—it may even be your spouse who has given up or feels that it is inappropriate for you to try to do anything to influence the Jewish identity of your grandchildren. Some friends or relatives may tell you that you are going about it the wrong way. Alternatively, they may suggest that you should leave your children and grandchildren alone to find their own direction in life. One way to avoid such confrontation and "advice" is to refrain from sharing your approach with others whose opinion does not interest you. (Because it lies heavy on our souls, we tend to speak about it often and indiscriminately.) Don't think that just because your other children may have married Jewish spouses or are raising Jewish children that they will be supportive of your efforts.

Claire, an older woman who approached me after I made a presentation at a community book fair held at a local Jewish Community Center, her face expressing a sense of despair, said, "My husband wouldn't even come to listen to what you had to say. He has given up. And he doesn't want me to do anything. My other children say that I am 'butting in' and it is none of my business what religious choices my children or grandchildren make. But I refuse to give up. The Jewish identity of my grandchildren is too important to me. I know that one day they will realize that it is important to them as well." Like many of her generation, Claire is caught between her desire for Jewish grandchildren and her reticence to do anything that will cause friction between her and her husband. She also worries about damaging her relationship with her other children or placing an obstacle in the relationship that her adult children have with one another. But she allows neither reason to dissuade her.

Claire has realistic concerns that have to be weighed against an investment in the Jewish future. Her optimism is instructive to all of us. The children of interfaith families represent an opportunity for us to grow the Jewish community that we have to actively and passionately seize.

Sidney understands this for sure. A proud Jewish grandpa, he refused to give up. When I met him after a stint as a scholar-in-residence at his synagogue, he recounted to me the numerous "incidents"—as he calls them—that he had with his adult children regarding Judaism and his grandchildren. Each time he tried something, his children reacted negatively. Finally, they did accept his "gift" to send the grandkids to Jewish summer camp. And he says he knew it was all worth it when one of the kids (by then a sophomore in college) said to him; "Grandpa, thanks. I know that Mom and Dad did not make it easy for you. But that's okay, 'cause I never made it easy for them. But I wanted to let you know that while I think they were afraid to make a religious choice for me, you will be pleased to know that I have made one for myself. I have *chosen* to be a Jew."

Jewish identity is not static. Rather, it is dynamic. It does not follow a straight path. Yours probably didn't. There is no reason to think that your grandchildren's will either. Thus, no matter what you confront, remember that there is always the possibility that your grandchildren will eventually embrace their Jewish identity—make sure that you leave the door open for them to do so.

4. WEAR YOUR OWN JEWISH IDENTITY PROUDLY.

There are all kinds of reasons to be proud to be Jewish. Perhaps it is because of the overwhelming number of Jewish Nobel Prize laureates and their accomplishments in disparate fields like science and medicine. Or maybe it is because of the Jewish contributions to culture, including the arts and entertainment. Possibly it is because of the notion of a Sabbath that ancient Judaism gave to an overworked world. Or the fact that the Hebrew Bible is also the foundational text for Christianity and Islam. It might even be the role that Israel plays as a democratic foothold in the Middle East. Or maybe it is something that you feel in your heart—although hard to explain or articulate. Whatever the reason, it is clear that the Jewish community has made its mark on civilization throughout its history and continues to do so.

Because of the increasingly antiquated stigma of intermarriage as marrying *out* of Judaism and therefore "betraying" the Jewish community, some people are embarrassed to publicly acknowledge that their children have intermarried. They may be afraid of the social backlash among their friends. If they are active synagogue members or involved in the local Jewish Federation, they may be reticent to admit that such activity did not positively impact on the Jewish identity of their adult children, an identity which they gauge strictly—and incorrectly—by the barometer of whether or not their children have married someone who was not raised in the Jewish community. Besides recognizing that interfaith marriage is more an accident of demography and not necessarily a reflection of Jewish identity (we meet someone at school, at work, or in social contexts, and we fall in love), it is important to recognize that interfaith marriage only undermines one's Jewish identity *if* the Jewish community does not allow the individual to exercise it fully. So don't permit the way that segments of the organized Jewish community interpret the decisions your children have made to shape your own Jewish identity. In order to help nurture the Jewish identity of your grandchildren, it is essential that you wear your own Jewish identity especially proudly at this time in your life.

Some people participate actively in Jewish communal life when they have young children. Then, feeling that Jewish communal institutions, particularly synagogues, no longer serve their needs, they drop their membership and often opt out of the community as a result. Now that your child is older and married to someone who isn't Jewish, perhaps you feel that you really need the services or support that the Jewish community provides. It may be one of the reasons that you are reading this book. While activity in the Jewish community is not essential to having a strong Jewish identity, they normally go hand in hand—especially if you want to exhibit your Jewish identity for others, particularly for your grandchildren. But we understand how difficult it is to reconnect to the community through institutional Judaism. So what are some smaller initial steps you can take to display your proud Jewish identity?

You may want to begin simply by wearing a Star of David or ḥai necklace. For some, this may seem trite and inconsequential, but it quietly represents a public display of Judaism, Jewish allegiance and Jewish identity. It unabashedly tells people—including your grandchildren—who you are and where you see yourself in relation to the rest of the world. Moreover, it might be something that they will eventually want to wear, because it is yours. Perhaps they want to emulate you. I like to take this idea even one step further. I have a group of special ties that I wear only just before and during Ḥanukkah; the ties are in various styles, but all are decorated with dreidels and other relevant holiday symbols. They clearly communicate who I am to others.

Wearing your Jewish identity proudly is not limited to the clothing or jewelry you wear. It also includes how you express yourself verbally about the Jewish community. What you say about Jews (and even about Israel) reveals your attitude about the community and its institutions. It also helps to determine what people (particularly your grandchildren) think you feel about Judaism and your Jewish identity, and your connections to the Jewish community. As might be expected, the cornerstone institutions in the Jewish community, therefore, become pivotal in this regard: synagogue, Jewish Community Center, and Jewish Federation. But membership in any of these institutions—generally translated as paying dues—while an important step, is not enough. The critical question is the extent of participation inside and outside these institutions.

For the synagogue, it is about attending services and participating in holiday events, as well as social and educational programs. This may seem like a simple repetition of the company line, what you might expect to hear. And to some extent, admittedly, you are right. Where we differ is in the motivation. It is not enough to be motivated to attend services, for example, because you think it sets a good example for your grandchildren or because you feel an obligation to other members of the community (though both reasons are sufficiently valid). You should attend because you get something out of the experience. And if you don't, then work to change the experience. It is this effort, more than your mere attendance, that communicates loudly to others, because the experience is important enough for you to want to change it.

The same thing holds true for the Jewish Community Center, even though its focus is quite different. What JCC programs have in common is Jewish *peoplehood*. The fact that you want to spend social time with other Jews—whatever the reason, even when it is difficult to explain—is another important lesson to demonstrate to your grandchildren. While it would be nice to say that what sets the JCC basketball league apart from others is the inculcation of Jewish values, it would probably be an overstatement. So take an active role in the governance of the JCC and its policies. If there are policies, particularly those about making the institution more inclusive, work to change those policies. Your grandkids will see how that is important to you, too.

Finally, while the local Jewish Federation is mostly associated with raising money (the "campaign"), it is really about the redistribution of funds for the good of the community. And this is the essential understanding of *tzedakah* (loosely translated from the Hebrew as "charitable giving"). Your financial contribution to the local Federation, however modest it may be, demonstrates your affirmation of some basic Jewish principles: a belief in community; a belief in your responsibility to support the community and its members; and an affirmation of the principle that the community has a responsibility to redistribute the wealth of individuals (from those who have to those who need). While it may be politically incorrect to share with others the size of your gift to the Federation, it is not inappropriate to share with your grandchildren the fact that you give, that you give *regularly* (both of which you should do), and where the money goes. (You may even want to consider discussing "earmarking" a gift with your grandchildren so that you can together decide on an appropriate recipient.)

While these three institutions may provide you with a foundation for community involvement, your participation in community should not be limited to them. By participating in other institutions and organizations, you are able to demonstrate the extent of Jewish communal life to your grandkids. In addition, just as you may be more inclined to participate in other institutions, their interest may be similarly piqued. Not all of our needs or interests are served by the three familiar institutions mentioned above. Newer organizations within many local communities include Jewish museums, film festivals, cultural fairs, and book circles. They all invite easy participation and may also welcome volunteer assistance during various events. More traditional institutions might need volunteer help as well, such as Jewish Family and Children's Services.

Rather than thinking about involvement in the community as a series of overlapping concentric circles, think of it as a group of independent circles. The goal is not merely to increase the number of circles. Rather, the goal is to deepen each circle and your participation in it. The deeper you go, the more meaningful the experience.

5. MODEL A WELCOMING ATTITUDE TOWARD ALL.

Abraham had it right—at least, as Jewish tradition and the Bible like to tell it. He left the flaps of his tent open on all sides so that he could see visitors coming from afar, regardless of the direction from which they came. Then he would go out to greet them. When people come to visit us in our homes, we anticipate their visit in various ways. If it is nighttime, we may leave the front light on. Regardless of the time of day, we make sure that there are no obstacles in their path. And we frequently go outside—even in foul weather—to welcome them in, often before they reach our front door. Some friends, referred to as "backdoor friends," feel so much at home that they don't use the front door (considering it too formal) and may even just walk inside without knocking. Once inside, we offer our guests food and drink and make sure that they are comfortable in our homes. We may use our best dishes—reserved only for special guests. Each of us probably has some way of distinguishing how we treat guests and visitors as compared to how we interact with the members of our family or those who live in our homes. When we treat our guests well, they will want to come back and visit often. (Unfortunately, we also know how to treat people when we don't want them to come back and visit.) We can also be assured that our guests will share their experience of our hospitality with others.

At this point you may be saying to yourself, "What does this have to do with making sure that my grandchildren will identify with the Jewish community?" It's actually a rather simple formula. The approach we take for honored guests in our homes (and all guests should be honored according to Jewish tradition) should be extended as a model of welcoming into our synagogues and other Jewish communal institutions as well. For these institutions are extensions of our homes and of ourselves. Likewise, why would your grandchildren want to be part of a community that excludes them, or at least excludes one of their parents? When your grandchildren see that you are indeed welcoming to all, welcoming to *both* of their parents, and particularly the parent (and his/her family) who is not Jewish, your grandchildren will want to emulate your inviting approach to visitors. In particular, your adult child's non-Jewish partner needs to feel unconditionally welcome. As a result, you will reduce the tension between your adult child and his/her partner. Share well-kept family recipe secrets. Invite them to participate in sports and social activities with you one on one, without your child or grandchildren. Try to be as flexible as you can with your time, and always keep the hypothetical doors to your "tent" open.

For example, Kerry's kids always knew that they could invite their friends for any meal, especially for Shabbat or holidays, without a warning. And once they left for college, they would bring their friends—and their friends' laundry—home for extended periods of time. This is the kind of atmosphere to foster in your home for your grandchildren. Don't make them feel that they have to make extensive arrangements if they want to visit. Be prepared to change your plans on a moment's notice for them. Don't fuss about where they sit, how they are dressed or where they leave their things. This is not the time to teach them *those* things. Just be happy that they are there—with you.

The same thing goes for your adult children. Unwittingly, when our adult children come to visit, we sometimes regress to the parenting roles that we had when they were young. If they are encouraged to bring their "childhood baggage" back into the house when they visit, such tension will color the interfaith tensions that may simmer under the surface of their visit and can inhibit your ability to nurture your grandchildren and their religious identity.

When this kind of welcoming attitude is also embodied by Jewish *institutions*, your grandkids will feel included there as well. They will see it as part of the tradition of Jewish community, a community of which they will proudly want to be part. Obviously, you have much more control over expressing a welcoming attitude in your home than in the Jewish institutions to which you may belong. But that's not to say you have *no* control over those Jewish institutions. Even if you are just a "regular" member, not serving on a board or a committee, you can still make your voice heard. Your opinions matter, and your actions speak even louder. Almost every Jewish institution has one or several members who take it upon themselves to be the most welcoming, most friendly souls for the newcomers who walk through the doors. Even if you are not an outgoing type, if you are a "regular" at an institution and you see a new face, a simple "Hello, how are you, I like it here, I hope you do, too" will go a huge distance in making a newcomer feel welcome. Don't let people sit alone during services or programs or stand alone during receptions.

Whatever the issues are that you might seek to change within a Jewish institution, odds are strong that you are not alone in seeking that change. Sometimes written policies are a barrier, but more often it's the unspoken attitudes that make a Jewish institution less welcoming than it could be. After all, an institution is really only a composite of its membership. And we know that you can find like-minded allies among the other members in your quest to make a beloved institution more welcoming toward your intermarried children and your grandchildren and all intermarried families. Together you can work to create a more welcoming community.

6. *I*F YOUR SON-IN-LAW OR DAUGHTER-IN-LAW IS HELPING TO RAISE A JEWISH CHILD, CELEBRATE THOSE ACTIONS.

Regardless of the background of your son/daughter-in-law, if he or she is helping to raise a Jewish child, that should be celebrated—supported, encouraged, thanked, appreciated—very little of which is normally done by us, either as members of the family or as a Jewish community in general. These men and women are the unsung heroes of their generation. They come from different traditions and religious backgrounds, yet are sharing their greatest gifts with us—their children, your grandchildren. Few of us would be able to do the same, were the roles reversed. Appreciating their sacrifices, encouraging their efforts, and supporting their Jewish decisions shows them (and the community at large) that we have an optimistic vision for the Jewish future.

Take advantage of the calendar to say thank you, especially on Mother's Day or Father's Day. While some may feel that these are special days that have been created by greeting-card companies, they have become embedded in the American calendar. In a sense, therefore, they have become part of American "civil religion." Unlike holidays that may originate in Jewish or

31

Christian religion, they are fairly neutral. When you celebrate your son- or daughter-in-law—and the actions that he or she has taken to acknowledge the Jewish heritage of the children, your grandchildren are being celebrated as well. Each Jewish identity spark needs to be fanned so that eventually it can fully ignite.

Optimism is not a feeling often associated with interfaith marriage in the Jewish community. Perhaps you remember a time when intermarriage was a very rare occurrence, and if it did happen, it was seen as Jews "marrying out," lost forever to the Jewish community. Some families would even say *kaddish* and sit *shiva* for their intermarried children, mourning them as dead. Those days are long gone. Today, although we may feel challenged about this generation's rapid rise in intermarriage rates, we also know that there is nothing automatic about interfaith marriages or the way intermarried couples raise their children. And while some may still use language like "marrying out," we prefer to think of the opportunities inherent in so many wonderful young people "marrying in" to the Jewish community. The way we welcome them and support them can make all the difference in the world. Rather than losing a child who has married someone who is not Jewish, we have to begin to think about the inherent potential in gaining the one whom our child has married. This notion is similar to the idea that we have not lost a son/daughter in marriage. Rather, we have gained a daughter/son.

Moving to an optimistic, supportive mindset may not be so easy. Unfortunately, one of the typical Jewish stereotypes is our never-ending pessimism. We do too much complaining and indulging in self-pity about the state of our personal Jewish affairs and just not enough celebrating. One historian even calls it a lachrymose approach to Jewish history. There is a famous essay called "The Ever Dying People." It seems to be part of the pattern that Jewish people have followed since the very beginning of our history. What did our forbears do after witnessing the amazing miracles that led them out of slavery in Egypt and through a parted sea to freedom? They almost immediately started *kvetching* (complaining) that they were going to die in the desert! It was too hot. There was insufficient food and water. The walk was too arduous. It was better to be slaves in Egypt, said some. At least there we knew what to expect.

Not that we should forget the unmatched suffering of the Jewish people through the millennia, but with that history in mind we can see that the current generation of Jews is the most educated, most socially affluent in history. We live a free society that has given us endless opportunities and choices, but we still complain. Instead of looking at our successes, we allow the challenges that we face to eclipse everything else. It is what we like to call the "ain't it awful" syndrome. This has to stop. The only way to grow is through optimism. After all, who would want to cast his or her lot with a people that can't paint a bright future for itself? And who would want to raise children amid such negativity?

Don't just wait for something you perceive as positively nurturing the Jewish identity of your grandchildren to happen before showing your appreciation to your son/daughter-in-law. Instead, express yourself frequently. Don't be afraid to be effusive with your praise. Compliment and support his or her attempts to engage the Jewish community as an individual, not just in the role of parent of Jewish children. And make sure that the son/daughter-in-law is aware of the advocacy role you play on his or her behalf in the community. It is important to feel welcomed and accepted by you—and the community—rather than merely tolerated as a social phenomenon that has to be dealt with irrespective of how large it is. This may also make it easier for the non-Jewish parent to take those actions.

Maryanne told us about the support she receives from her Jewish in-laws. The warmest moments have come during life-cycle events like her daughter's bat mitzvah, when the pride in her in-laws' faces spoke even louder than their kind words. But on a deeper level, Maryanne points to the little things in her relationship with her in-laws that have helped her grow more comfortable raising Jewish children even though she herself was raised Episcopalian. "They never made me feel stupid" is how she describes it. "They seemed genuinely excited about sharing their Judaism. They made it fun, and often they made it funny, because they have such a great sense of humor."

Of course, celebrating is the easy part. Nurturing is more of a challenge. Maryanne and her husband Richie had also had painstaking negotiations over her desire to retain her family tradition of putting up a Christmas tree during the holidays. Finally realizing all the sacrifices Maryanne would be making to raise their children Jewish, Richie relented, though he dreaded his parents' reaction and actually kept it secret from them for the first few years of the marriage. It was only after their first child's *brit* and after they joined a synagogue that

Richie agreed to have his parents over during the holidays, because he felt "armed with enough ammunition" for the argument he felt sure would ensue. And when his parents arrived they did indeed seem surprised to see a tree, and Maryanne could clearly identify disappointed looks on their faces. "Oh, I didn't know you had a Christmas tree" was all Richie's mom said.

"It connects me to my parents," Maryanne responded. Her father had passed away several years earlier. She then pointed out a number of ornaments that had special meaning to her from her childhood, as well as those that were actually older than she was and had belonged to her grandparents. To Richie's surprise, there was no ensuing argument, and not even comments made to him privately. His parents apparently decided to take a "wait and see" attitude and instead focused on the positive steps Maryanne had already taken toward Judaism. After all, during that very same visit she served them Hanukkah latkes she had cooked based on a recipe her mother-in-law had recommended. Instead of complaining about the Christmas tree, her mother-in-law spent the night fawning over the latkes.

Looking back, Maryanne greatly appreciates the emphasis on the positive that her in-laws always maintained. Their optimism and their celebration of Jewish life contributed greatly to her being able to raise the next generation of Jews. Without that kind of support, she doubts her children would feel as Jewishly connected as they do today. She also realized that the Christmas tree ceased to have the same meaning it once had. For a few years after she let go of the tree she continued to display her family's ornaments. These eventually gave way to the children's H̲anukkah *menorot* made in Hebrew School—and to the *menorot* that her in-laws gave her and asked that she pass them on to the grandchildren and those who come after.

7. *B*E HONEST AND OPEN WITH YOUR GRANDCHILDREN ABOUT YOUR FEELINGS WITHOUT "GUILTING" THEM OR THEIR PARENTS.

You've probably heard this statement, but we think that it warrants repeating: nothing is impossible in a supportive environment. While it is challenging to create and maintain such an environment, it is crucial to developing and sustaining a good relationship with your grandchildren. And it is within such a relationship that you'll best be able to help nurture the Jewish identity of your grandchildren. Key to this approach are honesty and openness *without* guilt.

Celebrating Jewish choices (as discussed in the previous chapter) is just one aspect of this open flow of feelings. There are challenges in being Jewish, too, and we shouldn't shy away from discussing them. What you say and do will undoubtedly evolve as your grandchildren grow older. So be sensitive to their age. As a so-called authority figure, you say things that make an impression on young children. You can talk to them about Jewish identity and what it means to you. (Indeed, what does it mean to you? Think deeply about it. Stay away from abstract concepts or "party lines" that you are simply repeating. Be simple and concrete. Try to recall how you felt when you were their age.) As they get older, you may be able to talk to them about the personal challenges you feel with regard to their Jewish identity. (Don't forget that adolescents reject authority in general and instead take their lead from peers. This has nothing to do with their Jewish identity or lack thereof.)

It may be tempting, but don't force your grandchildren to fulfill the disappointments you may have with your own adult children, particularly regarding their Jewish identity. And as we have said before, the Jewish identity of your adult children should not be measured by whom they married. Be especially careful not to use your grandchildren to get to your children or to put them in the middle of a relationship with your children. Remember, you represent a gateway into Judaism for your grandkids, but you can't force them to walk through that portal. They have to choose it. Think of yourself as an ambassador into Jewish life. As in the world of diplomacy, communication is expressed through thoughtful words and deeds, but also through body language and unspoken cues. Likewise, look for those cues in your children and grandchildren. The goal is to help them make connections and find meaning, not to force them to go through the motions of Jewish ritual in order to make *you* happy.

While it is a common stereotype (and perhaps one with some real substance) that Jewish mothers use guilt to manipulate the behavior of others, especially their children, it is extremely important that you avoid such a posture with your adult children and grandchildren. Guilt is not a positive Jewish value.

Nor will it help you bring about the task at hand. Not only will "guilting" not accomplish the desired result; you will probably succeed in pushing them further from you. The application of guilt will place additional strain on your relationship and make nurturing the Jewish identity of your grandchildren more difficult, if not impossible.

Honesty is a much more powerful tool than guilt. We're talking about an open and ongoing dialogue. To learn more about your grandkids, let them learn more about you and find common interests that can serve as entryways into a stronger Jewish identity. For example, our friend Joseph's lifelong love affair with baseball has infected his son and grandchildren. They make it a tradition to visit Joseph at his home in Florida each year to attend spring training games. There was nothing inherently Jewish in this activity until a convergence of two recent events. First, the L.A. Dodgers' Jewish all-star Shawn Green decided to sit out an important game on Yom Kippur, which Joseph discussed with his grandkids by telling them that Shawn Green is now his "new favorite player." Then Joseph found out that a company produced a set of trading cards of every Jewish major-leaguer in history, which he promptly bought for his grandkids as a Hanukkah gift.

At the family's holiday gathering, Joseph made "a big production" about giving them the trading cards. The card on top was, of course, Shawn Green, because the kids know him. Joseph then pulled out two more cards: Hank Greenberg and Sandy Koufax. The reverence he held for these two men was immediately apparent, and as he began to talk about what they meant to him, the rest of the room fell quiet. He told how, as a young boy, he and his family and the entire community felt electrified when they heard about Greenberg's decision not to play on Yom Kippur. Joseph tried to explain how life in the 1940s was very different for Jews, about how fans yelled slurs at Greenberg throughout his career. And how Greenberg's congregation spontaneously stood up and gave him a standing ovation on that holiest day of the year. Then he talked about what pitcher Koufax did, skipping Game One of the World Series because it, too, fell on Yom Kippur. Talking about these men as his heroes, Joseph nearly choked up and in doing so turned these simple trading cards into family heirlooms that his grandkids will cherish forever.

One piece of information that Joseph also knew but did not impart was the fact that Hank Greenberg, like his own son, had married a woman who was not of the Jewish faith, and that Greenberg's children never considered themselves Jewish. Joseph omitted that bit because the story is about Jewish pride, not a warning from the past. And because that's not the case with his own family. When Hank Greenberg intermarried in the 1940s, it really did mean "marrying out." Today, thankfully, things are different. Joseph considers his non-Jewish daughter-in-law as "married in." His positive embrace of his grandchildren is based on enthusiasm and pride about being Jewish, and like his love of baseball, it's contagious.

8. $\mathcal{S}$EPARATE THE DIFFICULTIES IN YOUR RELATIONSHIP WITH YOUR CHILD FROM THE RELATIONSHIP YOU WANT TO NURTURE WITH YOUR GRANDCHILDREN.

All relationships include some difficulties. Only perfect relationships do not have any difficulties—and they are among the most dysfunctional! So always beware of perfection. While such relationships may find their ways into novels and in movies, perfection just doesn't exist in real human relationships. Remember that while some may see their children's choice of non-Jewish spouses as a rejection of them and their ties to Judaism (and there are some that may, in fact, be so), most interfaith marriages are *not* an acting out of adult children against their parents, nor are they a rejection of Judaism or the Jewish community. Rather, generally, they are simply a matter of two people meeting and falling in love. Sometimes, however, it is difficult for parents to separate the difficulties that they may have in their relationship with their children from the fact that they have married someone from a different religion (even when, as in most cases, that religion is no longer actively practiced). As a result, the interfaith component in

41

the parent-child relationship seems to eclipse all else. In some cases it is even blamed for the difficulty *in* the parent-child relationship. This may make it easier for parents because it allows them to push any blame onto their children and away from themselves without taking any responsibility. And in some measure we all bear responsibility for the problems in our relationships.

As difficult as it is, make yourself aware of the relationship between your child's marital decision and a possible rejection of your value system. Is there one? Or does your non-Jewish son- or daughter-in-law actually reflect your value system quite well, even though he or she doesn't share your ethnic or cultural or religious heritage? Your relationship with your kids and your grandkids has the potential to worsen—and often does—when you allow the difficulties between you and your children to spill over into the relationship you are trying to nurture with your grandchildren. And this could happen without your even realizing it.

As I watched the relationship evolve between Sam and son through the years, it was clear to me—but seldom to Sam— that this father and son never had a good relationship. Jack's marriage to a Roman Catholic woman, although not an acting out or rejection of family values, was clearly read by Sam as such. For Sam, any problem was a direct result of Jack and Sue's interfaith marriage. He refused to see it as anything else and certainly would not take any responsibility. It didn't matter that Sue did not push her personal faith onto her husband or children. Admittedly Jack was not interested in Judaism or any organized religion. So he was not interested in passing on

Judaism to his children either. Anything Jewish that was promoted in the home was at Sue's insistence, for she understood the importance of raising children with religious values.

We all know how attuned to their surroundings children can be, even the youngest children, and even to the subtlest of human interactions. Tensions—especially those that are unspoken—are still transmitted, albeit through body language and hurt feelings. Your relationship with your grandchildren may be separate, yet it is inevitably tied to how you get along with your children.

In many families, the birth of a grandchild is the "excuse" we've been waiting for to reconcile (or if not reconcile, than at least set aside) outstanding issues. This was the case with James, who couldn't help but feel that his son had betrayed him by marrying a woman from Korea. James wasn't vocal about his feelings. In fact, he tried his best to be supportive of the young couple. But his nagging sense of loss inevitably rose to the surface of their relationship and, as a result, created tension between James and his son. And if James sensed the tension, it's safe to assume his children—including his daughter-in-law—did as well. However, the birth of his first grandchild, a boy, took James completely by surprise. He could not have anticipated how he felt as a grandparent and how it changed the way he felt toward his son and daughter-in-law. Perhaps it was a result of the decision that James' son and daughter-in-law made to have the baby circumcised in a *brit milah* ceremony. This alleviated some of James' fears about the child's Jewish identity. According to James, however, this was about more than just the religious identity of the child. Becoming a grandfather affirmed for him the permanence of his son's marriage, as well as the notion of his own legacy. His recognition of these feelings also drew him closer to his daughter-in-law.

Emboldened by a new outlook, now James' concern is about resolving any residual tension that remains between his children and him. He knows that "the air is not fully clear," but the lines of communication—and of love—have been reopened. James has even raised himself to the point of being able to actually thank his daughter-in-law for giving him a Jewish grandchild.

The process of reconciliation is not over for James and his son or daughter-in-law, but they are all on the right road. James confided in me that he knows that it is a lifelong process, and although he may not be good at it, he is working hard on it. Too much is riding on it for him to do anything less.

For others, the birth of a grandchild may not be enough to melt away the tensions of past disagreements. Of this we can be sure: If left unattended, these tensions will erode any positive relationship you might still have with your children and is likely to prevent the development of a relationship with your grandchildren. Attend to the tensions even if they remain unresolved. Honest, nonjudgmental dialogue continues to be the best approach. So approach your son or daughter with one thing in mind: Let's start talking.

9. $\mathcal{S}$HARE STORIES AND MEMENTOES FROM YOUR JEWISH PAST.

One of the best ways to assist young children in establishing a connection to their Jewish identity is to help them forge a link with a Jewish past. This anchors them in a well-defined group: the Jewish people. The more they feel directly connected to the Jewish people, the more they may feel as if they "belong." And abstract ideas are often best grasped in the form of stories. People relate more to things that are tangible than they do to ideas—and even more to the people who present them or relate to them. While it is true of people of any age, it is especially the case with children, because they have yet to develop the ability to reason abstractly. This is part of the natural process of maturation and parallels the process of growth and positive aging.

Some families have an abundance of religious artifacts and other items that have been handed down from one generation to the next. Other families even have articles that have accompanied their family's journey through history, especially as it migrated from community to community or country to country. All of these items are important vehicles to employ in our attempt to express this idea of belonging in a palpable way.

When visiting the Jewish community of Rome recently, Kerry marveled at the people he met—many of whom had local ties that went back two thousand years. They shared family stories, recipes, and religious items that had been handed down through the generations. But most of us do not have such items in our possession. While you may want to consider a plan to acquire such items periodically if you don't have them—especially those connected to the family celebration of holidays—now is the time to focus primarily on what you *do* have that is available to share with your grandchildren. (The Olitzky family tries to find something special in anticipation of each Jewish holiday to add to its collection. It can be something as simple as a string of lights for its *sukkah* or something to hold the *afikoman* when it is hidden for Passover, or as elaborate as an embroidered tablecloth for holiday use or an heirloom-quality Hanukkah *menorah*.)

If possible, begin telling the "story" of the Jewish family with photos (still, video, or digital) that capture the rhythm of the Jewish calendar and the Jewish life cycle with the full participation of family members. Visual images help children to place material items in context, especially since the idea of time is another one of those difficult abstract ideas for children to grasp. (You may want to keep this in mind when you take pictures in the future.) When you add your own personal commentary to describe the pictures, the stories of the photos come alive for children. When possible, select those photos that exhibit the involvement of those who are significant in the lives of your grandchildren, especially one of their parents. To see parents "doing Jewishly" when they were children is a vital image for children, especially because it may motivate them to want to emulate the activity undertaken by the parent in the photo.

Use the photos as a means to unobtrusively teach your grandchildren about Judaism and Jewish life without raising the possible ire of their parents. Some may consider this approach subversive. Others may call it clever and vital. Avoid any attempt to be didactic, unless specific things to be taught are requested by your grandchildren and supported by their parents. In other words, emphasize the "informal" in "informal education."

Rather than just sharing the images with your grandchildren, consider one or two things that you want to emphasize when showing the pictures to them. Take some time and do your planning before showing the snapshots or videos to the children. Rather than just giving them specific "how-to" details (such as "We light H̲anukkah candles at sunset" or "We light one more in succession for each night"), encourage their curiosity about Jewish ritual practices by asking them questions about the photograph or what is taking place in it. Such an approach will undoubtedly demand planning and preparation. So don't just say whatever comes to mind. Think carefully about what is important for them to learn, and isolate one or two things at a time.

There are two kinds of museums. The first is the one we are most accustomed to and were raised with: the look-but-don't-touch kind of museum. This is supposed to provide us insight into the past by showing it to us. The second museum model is one in which we play an interactive role. The museum is designed for us to engage the various things on display and actually places us in the context of the story told by the museum. In your approach to sharing the past with your grandchildren, opt for the second model rather than the first. It speaks of a living Judaism rather than one consigned to the past.

The activities displayed in the photographs do not have to reflect a traditional or what may be considered the classic approach to Jewish life. Nor should the photos be focused solely on Jewish religious and ritual practice, especially if it is not part of your family's culture or pattern of behaviors. It might be that your family has its own way of celebrating and expressing Judaism that is not specifically connected to the practice of Judaism as religion or its holidays. To be sure, most families do not look like the families that are idealized in religious school textbooks. Moreover, it should not be your goal to try to recreate some nostalgic form of *shtetl* Judaism. Your grandchildren will probably not relate to this approach at all. Instead, open them up to the possibilities of American Jewish life by showing them the way that their parents and other relatives engage Judaism. It is probable, nevertheless, that if the photos contain children doing Jewish things, that they probably are related to the basic celebration of holidays (e.g., playing *dreidel* or dressing up for Purim).

This approach to the past helps your grandchildren to "see the world through Jewish eyes," an idea made popular some years ago by Rabbi Howard Bogot. Such a concept may be difficult for your grandchildren to absorb, especially without the support of their parents. Nonetheless, it is critical to the development of their Jewish identity (and it's something that can happen naturally, without us having to necessarily name the process for them). If you are the only person actively nurturing such development, then it will be your responsibility to help them. In doing so, an object like grandma's wine glass, for example, emerges to become a *kiddish* cup rather than simply a piece of crystal, regardless of its origin or value. Why not prepare a scavenger hunt for your grandchildren prior to a trip or vacation? Include a variety of items that speak to them and their family and make sure that some things can be used (and described) as Jewish ritual items.

Jewish children's books are another way of sharing stories, especially if these books are among your favorites or from their parent's childhood. Make sure that these books are available when they come to visit, particularly during holiday periods if they highlight holiday observances and celebrations. Or you can bring them with you when you visit and read to them before they go to sleep. If you can place your own personal story from your family's past in relation to the book you are reading to your grandchildren, it adds a great deal of relevance for them and serves to support the Jewish identity you are trying to foster.

Obviously, if there are specific family items that you can actually give to your grandchildren or "store" for them until they get older, this will give them something to look forward to as they develop. Invite them to take a look at *their* candlesticks, for example, each time they come to visit. Don't be afraid to use these items, and let them actually handle them (unless they can get hurt). If you are visiting them, and it is relevant, bring the items with you to use and then return to their "storage place" when you return home. If they feel that the items are like those in a museum case and only from a distant past, they will not be able to relate to them very readily as children. So make sure that they get used.

While you will want to be sensitive to the age and gender of your grandchildren as you shape this approach, family recipes are another excellent way to excite them. Any time that their senses can be engaged (which is part of the intriguing impact of the Passover *seder*), we have a better chance of reaching people at any age. Our senses also have a stronger attachment to memory than do our cognitive faculties. As soon as we smell something familiar, for example, we are swept back to the other times we have experienced the same sensation. So take advantage of all that Jewish tradition and Judaism have to offer when providing your grandchildren with a *physical* connection to their Jewish past and a foundation for their Jewish future.

10. THROW THE BEST HOLIDAY PARTIES EVER.

We love the Jewish holidays, even those that are less than celebratory. If you look at the entire cycle of Jewish holidays, you can see the full spectrum of human emotions articulated in colorful and concrete ways. Too often holidays are relegated to the confines of the synagogue, where their planning and implementation is left to someone else. Or, more often, the holidays are completely ignored. But holidays are an important vehicle for connecting with the Jewish religious heritage, especially for young children. The challenge is to get in sync with the holiday calendar and share its rhythm with your grandchildren.

There are really two basic approaches. The first is to mark the holiday cycle as the holidays occur on the calendar. This is the classic approach. The second is to focus on those holidays that have the most resonance with your grandchildren, especially at young ages. These may also cause the least resistance from your children. In addition, they may be determined by when you have the chance to visit or interact with your grandchildren. However, note that it is important that the kids see you celebrate because *you* want to celebrate the holidays and not simply for their sake. With each passing year you can add holidays to the cycle, especially as they mature and are prepared for them.

So start with Passover. More North American families celebrate Passover in one way or another than any other Jewish holiday. Send out personal invitations. Perhaps the invitation can come from your grandchildren on your behalf. Rather than using a traditional *haggadah* or one that you may have received free from the local grocery store, use one of the new and innovative editions that have come out in recent years, or find a kid-friendly version, or better yet, take what you want from a group of *haggadot* and place the material in a loose-leaf notebook. Put a person's name on the cover of each notebook. (This is really for your grandchildren, but you will have to provide one for each person who attends.) Add new readings, games and activities to the notebook each year. Make sure that you include specific things that will speak to your grandchildren. Decorate your house accordingly. And if you are comfortable, dress up for the occasion. Maybe even provide masks for those around the table. "Plagues in a Bag" are fun props (for kids and adults) available through Judaica mail-order catalogs and JCC gift shops. One year Paul's family drew their own *seder* plates on special paper that was then mailed in and laminated, so that in the years following, the plates could be used for actual food and provide a wonderful memory and instant heirloom.

To keep everyone's attention, we like to start the *seder* in the most comfortable place in the house (usually the living room or family room). After all, we are no longer slaves and can eat wherever we want! Feel free to prepare vegetables to snack on (introduced at the appropriate time early in the *seder*). Then you can move to the dining room table for dinner. Stay away from frontal readings. Encourage participation and activities that involve as many *seder* guests as possible. Recite *Birkat ha-Mazon* (grace after meals) at the table. Then return to a comfortable place to finish, especially for after-*seder* singing and stories.

Even though Passover is a story about our Jewish ancestors, its message of freedom is universal and appeals to people of all backgrounds. That's why it is such a popular holiday, and why it presents an opportunity to create both a fun atmosphere for the grandkids and a welcoming atmosphere for their non-Jewish relatives. The Passover *seder* is built for the "first-timer" like no other holiday on the Jewish calendar. From the four questions to the explanation of each item on the *seder* plate, we have the chance to educate without talking down to our guests. Just keep in mind that if there *are* first-timers at your *seder*, it lowers barriers to translate all the Hebrew you might use (even the blessings).

For Hanukkah, the next-most-celebrated holiday on the Jewish calendar, we have eight consecutive opportunities to connect with our grandkids. While our inclination may be to push presents on the children, especially if we feel "competition" with grandparents from the other side of the family, extravagant presents are not really what leave a lasting impression on children. Can you name the gifts you got as a child? Probably not. It's the family, the food, and the fun times you had together that remain locked in your memory. Still, the excitement of giving and receiving is an undeniable part of the fun—even if the actual gifts won't be remembered—and we recommend that you try to give young children a little something on each of the eight nights, even if you only attend a Hanukkah party on one of the days of Hanukkah. It prolongs the joy for everyone involved.

Obviously, if you can be there to light candles with the kids for more than one night, that's even better. Let the holiday speak to the kids. And don't believe what people tell you—that Hanukkah is a minor festival, so you shouldn't make a big deal out of it. "Minor" is only related to the Jewish laws concerning what work can and can't be done on certain days. Hanukkah is and should be a major holiday in your life and the life of your grandchildren. How major you make it is totally up to you.

If you are hosting the Hanukkah celebration, begin with decorations. Yes, decorations. Fill your house with an expanding collection of *dreidels* and Hanukkah *menorot*. Enlist your grandchildren's help in searching out new ones for your growing collection as they travel. (Their arts and crafts projects should be encouraged and prominently displayed as well. If they aren't in a school that gives them the opportunity, make sure that you provide the materials and directions to do so. Post them on the refrigerator. Place them on the coffee table in your living room or use them as a centerpiece on your dining room table for the holidays. And don't let them do the projects by themselves. Join them.) Make sure there are plenty of Hanukkah books around the house, too (more stories and fewer explanations of the ritual and history of the holiday).

As for synagogue-based holiday celebrations, many of us share early childhood memories of watching our grandfathers mysteriously *daven* on the High Holidays or on Shabbat morning. It's a powerful, even spiritual image for us, and yet the beauty of that image may overpower the reality of those days, which also included—let's be honest—seemingly endless hours of boredom broken only by running around crazily with the other kids on the synagogue grounds or in the lobby. While there are now some excellent programs for children that take place concurrent with adult worship services, the truth is that most holidays in the traditional synagogue setting offer little stimulation for young children unless it's part of a regular and cherished family routine. If it only happens once a year, it can seem more like punishment than worship or celebration.

There is one glaring exception to this rule: the holiday of Purim. Purim is the most kid-friendly synagogue-based holiday on the Jewish calendar, and it might also serve as a much better first step into *shul* life for your non-Jewish son- or daughter-in-law than the High Holidays. On Purim they'll see the genuine joy in their children's celebration. Who can forget the excitement hanging on every spoken word of the *Megillah* until the rabbi tries to slip a "Haman" past us and we let loose with our *groggers* until the synagogue elders have to beg us to settle down? Or the costumes that, some say, can determine a child's future personality, based on whether they chose to dress like Vashti or Esther, Mordecai or King Ahasuerus. The *hamantashen* we enjoy afterwards are a fun reminder that Purim, like Passover and Hanukkah, also fits the classic formula of "They tried to kill us, we won, let's eat!"

Whatever the holiday, make it something that they will remember. Take lots of pictures and share them regularly throughout the year, reminding them of the terrific time that you had together—and make plans for the following year. Send them things during the year in anticipation of the holiday and what they have to look forward to, making sure to include the steps of preparation and planning you will be taking along the way.

11. *D*ISCUSS AGE-APPROPRIATE JEWISH CURRENT EVENTS WITH YOUR GRANDCHILDREN.

Whoever first suggested the etiquette rule about not discussing "money, religion or politics" around the dinner table was clearly *not* eating in a Jewish household! Politics in particular has been a passionate issue for Jews in America for at least a hundred years, and supporting the modern state of Israel has been an equally important concern for more than half a century. For many of us, the first thing we do when we read a newspaper is look for what's happening in Israel—and to Jewish communities around the world. This may be something we learned from watching our parents or perhaps a memory of our grandparents. Or it might be something that we shaped on our own over time. But what is clear is that the nurturing of an evolving Jewish identity is intimately wrapped up with current events. That is why we think it is so important to discuss current events regularly with members of your family, especially your grandchildren.

Obviously, what you discuss and how you discuss it will be determined by the age of your grandchildren and the context in which the discussion takes place. If you see them regularly, you will be able to do things differently than if you speak to them on the telephone. But a discussion of current events can be part of your regular conversation, something that they expect and look forward to. Since such a conversation should not be contrived, it is helpful if you can share part of yourself or something related to personal or family memory when discussing the current event.

For example, in the case of Israel, if you've been lucky enough to visit there you can share photos and memories with your grandkids, to paint a fuller picture than they may receive from news coverage that tends to focus exclusively on violent events—or to follow up on what they may have heard or read. (Obviously, if you can take them with you on your visit, or finance their own trip as a gift, that's really the best way to give them a new perspective on a place so central to Jewish identity.) If you've always discussed the news from Israel with your grown children, your grandkids will grow up in an environment where they come to associate you with that topic. If, however, your children don't share your interests and you can't engage them in conversation about Israeli current events, it may come as an abrupt non sequitur when you finally feel your grandkids are old enough to discuss it. Still, if it's important to you, try to find positive entry points into a conversation. Learn what they already know and how they feel about it. You can send them clippings from the newspaper with notes that are relevant, like "When I visited Israel …" or "My friend Joe lives near this place…." And don't forget to call their attention to things you see or read on the Internet. Without pushing—or teaching a lesson plan—let them know why it's relevant to you and may be interesting to them.

Historically, one of the most amazing aspects of the abstract concept we call "Jewish peoplehood" is the connection Jews feel with other Jews around the world despite never having met personally. It is this connection, compassion, and concern that we want to pass on to our grandchildren, so they, too, feel part of the Jewish people. With today's modern communications it's easier than ever to find news about Jewish struggles and successes around the globe. Whether it's pride in the first Israeli athlete to win Olympic gold, concern about terror victims, or interest in the latest (inevitable) Jewish Nobel Prize winner, we wear it on our sleeves, and we should share it with our grandkids.

A challenge, however, arises if our *only* connection to Judaism is ethnic pride. Peoplehood is a broader concept than ethnicity. Your grandchildren—as children of intermarriage—will share at least two ethnicities, maybe more. If the only connection to Judaism we offer them is through ethnicity, it will inevitably be a tenuous connection. We live in a very different world than that of, say, Brooklyn in the 1950s, when you didn't have to do a single religious act and yet were still totally immersed in Jewish life. Today the connections we offer through Jewish peoplehood must transcend ethnicity. What this "post-ethnic Judaism" will look like is anybody's guess—it's still being created! And willing or not, we are all participants in its creation, so let's make it a positive step forward.

For your grandkids, this may mean picking and choosing the current events we discuss based on their transcendence over ethnicity. For example, Israel is the only country in history to move tens of thousands of Africans to within its own borders—not to become slaves but rather to become immediate and equal citizens. That's something to be proud of (without minimizing the challenges these immigrants still face within Israeli society). The diversity of Israeli society is always one of the most surprising finds for first-time visitors to the country. This might be especially relevant if your grandchildren are multiracial Jews.

Likewise, just pointing out Jewish celebrities—playing the "Who's a Jew" game—may or may not evoke feeling of connection within your grandchildren. Perhaps it's not enough for those celebrities to "be"; perhaps they have to "do" Jewish as well. Senator Joseph Lieberman's Judaism was not peripheral to his presidential campaign; it's a central part of his identity. A number of today's movie stars, like Adam Sandler, Ben Stiller, and Natalie Portman, identify publicly and proudly as Jews in ways that stars in eras past never did. Sandler's famous "Hanukkah Song" is arguably one of the largest boosts to Jewish pride in America since the Six Day War!

If keeping tabs on popular culture is not of interest to you, look for other "points of intersection" between your interests and those of your grandkids. Even local politics often has a Jewish angle to it. And certainly some of the major issues that are emerging in national politics have a Jewish take, especially as the federal government gets involved with end-of-life-issues, stem cell research, and faith-based initiatives. Current events can tie Jews together and strengthen Jewish identity, but only when the events are personally relevant. Knowing something's very important to their grandparents may make that connection for your grandkids and encourage them to pay attention to some important Jewish current events, and that may in turn build a lifetime interest for them. Asking your grandchildren to be on the lookout for something that you have identified as being of interest to you is a great place to start.

12. MAKE SURE THAT YOUR HOME IS "OBVIOUSLY" JEWISH.

While it may be difficult to discern the abstract values that make a home Jewish, it is a lot easier to isolate those values when they can be found in concrete forms. That is the real reason why it is important to adorn your home Jewishly. And it is particularly important when you want to communicate these values—in their concrete forms—to your grandchildren.

Besides the usual objects that are associated with rituals (such as a Hanukkah *menorah* and Shabbat candlesticks), you may want to consider other items. In Kerry's home, for example, there is a collection of Noah's arks. Not only was this tied into the Noah story in the Bible, but it also provided an impetus for his children as they were growing older to be on the lookout for Noahs wherever they went. The connection to the home can be strengthened in such a way.

Luckily, the presentation of every Jewish ritual object imaginable has been raised to an art form. From Hanukkah *menorot* and *dreidels*, Passover plates and *matzah* covers, Shabbat candleholders and *havdalah* spice boxes, many families have more than one of each or even a whole collection. Artisans from Israel and around the world offer a dizzying array of beautiful, imaginative, and sometime even bizarre variations on Jewish ritual objects. As we discussed earlier, displaying these items may help you tell your Jewish story. But what about actually using them?

Take the *mezuzah*, for example. Hebrew for "doorpost," it serves as a proud and clear indicator right next to your front door that this is a Jewish home. It's impossible to guess how many tens of thousands of *mezuzah* variations are available for purchase, but we feel pretty safe in suggesting that there's at least one out there to meet your tastes. What's not different in all those variations is the central message contained on the scroll inside (which is far more important than the decorative case that surrounds and protects the scroll): "Hear O Israel, the Eternal is our God, the Eternal is One." The *Shema*, the timeless Jewish "rallying cry," is the ultimate expression of the Jewish people. While the prayers for candle lighting or breaking bread might be easier to share with young children, as your grandkids grow old enough to absorb more abstract concepts, the *Shema* is perhaps the most important and powerful prayer for them to know. And the *mezuzah* may be the conversation starter that allows you to discuss it. It is easy to make the connection between the *Shema* that is in the *mezuzah* and the *Shema* that is said at night before going to sleep, especially if you get the chance to speak to your grandchildren at night before bedtime. (And look how many grandchildren spend the night at their grandparents' home at least once in a while.)

Again, these conversations should come about organically. If you sit down and try to deliver a lesson plan, it may come off as stilted. But in order for a casual conversation around a *mezuzah* to happen, you have to actually *have* a *mezuzah* on your door! If possible, place a *mezuzah* on your front door and on every door.

And if you move into a new home or you get the opportunity to affix a new *mezuzah*, invite your grandchildren to help you. If there is a bedroom in the house reserved for a particular grandchild, invite that child to help you select the *mezuzah*. Some people even place the *mezuzah* below its required height so that small children can see it and kiss it when they enter. If your grandchildren see you express yourself with the *mezuzah* (kissing it when you enter your home or other homes), they will see that you don't take it for granted—and perhaps they shouldn't either.

Prominently display the ritual objects you use regularly. And if you don't use them regularly, there is no better time than now to start. Make sure that the *kiddush* cup and Shabbat candlesticks shine and are on public display, not hidden away in some cabinet. Be sure to share the stories behind each object with your grandchildren: when it was acquired and how it has been used.

But ritual objects are not enough. They are associated with the religion of Judaism. For your grandchildren to fully understand your relationship with Judaism and how much it means to you, Jewish culture should permeate the environment in which you live.

Consider the books that are on the nightstand next to your bed. What are you reading? And what about the books on the coffee table in your living room? And the magazines and newspapers in the rack in the family room? And as for children's books, what are the titles that you keep on hand? Of course, as people who stand with one foot each in a different world, there should be a mix of secular and Jewish, of the everyday and the sacred. But too often, the everyday fully eclipses the sacred. Your reading should reflect the items discussed in the previous section (regarding Jewish current events.) And don't forget to have age-appropriate books about the holidays on hand when they visit, encouraging them to take them home, should they want to do so.

As for art, what is displayed on your walls? What pieces of art have you collected in your travels? And what is displayed in the room your grandchildren spend their time when they come to visit? We know how distorted an image of Israel most people have if they've never been there, because they only have media portrayals to rely on. Art and photography are fine ways to show the true beauty of the Jewish homeland. And if your grandchildren have expressed an interest in a particular art form, then make sure that you have available examples of Jewish-themed articles in that form. Use the art form as a way to enter into a conversation of the Jewish themes that are reflected in the art.

There are countless other cultural expressions of your Judaism that you may simply take for granted: the food you eat, the music you listen to, the celebrities you admire, the news stories you follow. If being Jewish is a natural part of your being, there will be ample opportunities to discuss Judaism with your grandchildren and help them understand what it is that you admire so much about our accomplishments as a people. It won't require such a clear articulation, however. They will simply absorb it by being around you.

13. COMMUNICATE REGULARLY WITH YOUR GRANDCHILDREN.

Martin Buber said it this way: "Real life is meeting." He meant it as a way of helping people to understand that meaningful life is established through relationships and that relationships are built through personal interactions. Developing relationships is not easy. Developing relationships long distance is even more difficult. That is why regular communication with your grandchildren—in a multiplicity of forms—is so important.

But it is also crucial that they know you are interested in everything that occupies their time and their interests. This means that you can't focus the conversation on their Jewish activities—or lack of them—even if your time to discuss things with the kids is limited. Only in the context of a conversation about other things will it be fruitful to introduce issues related to the nurturing of their Jewish identity.

It is a good idea to have a regularly scheduled time to speak to your grandchildren. This allows them to look forward to your call. This is especially important for younger children, whose ability to conceptualize time is limited by their age. While you might think that a few days or even a week is not a long time, it may seem like a year for most kids. That is why it is important that communication, even if it is brief, is frequent. Similarly, don't limit your calls to the times that you have reserved.

Check in with them when they have returned home from school, especially when they have some down time and may be looking for some conversation. Your adult children may even appreciate it! Stay away from questions like "How was school?" or "What did you learn today?" Ask more pointed questions about specific subjects or assignments or projects or relationships.

It is helpful to link the calls and communication to something that you want to emphasize. Some grandparents find that calling late on Friday afternoon or early Friday evening, before dinner, before Shabbat, is a good time. As a result, the grandchildren begin to associate Friday evening (and Shabbat) with the times they talk with their grandparents. This becomes a positive memory associated with the marking of Shabbat even when little else might be done in their homes.

If you are not computer-savvy, or have not mastered the technique of electronic communications, now is the time to develop a mastery of e-mail at least, and instant messaging or cell phone text messaging if you really want to impress the kids. These informal exchanges are among the best ways to maintain a regular dialogue with pre-teens—even if it is in the midst of their multi-tasking communication with their friends online. These media have quickly overtaken the letter. You can also send them electronic greeting cards periodically. If you send regular e-mails, you don't need to wait for them to correspond in return. Just keep them coming. E-mail is a great way to spread jokes and humorous photos; the good ones make the rounds and serve as a way to get your own personality across (depending on which you forward and which you filter out). Even if you live next door, electronic communication is an essential way to reach the younger generation. Family members e-mail each other from within the same house!

Try to stay abreast of advances in electronic communication. Solicit the help of the grandkids you are trying to reach.

If you want a more "physical" connection over long distances, send packages regularly. Even if you only include one small item, your packages should be sent frequently. Vary the contents of the packages so that the kids won't know what to expect and possibly tire of what you send. Include items that reflect their interest, and along the way you can include things relevant to Jewish holidays and the like. But don't just send them. Send them with loving suggestions like "Once you finish these arts and crafts projects, send one to me so that I can display it in my living room and show all of my friends how great an artist you are." Then take a picture of what they sent and where you placed it and send that to them. Get the idea?

If you bake, send your baked goods. Paul's grandmother used to send her "world-famous" chocolate chip cookies and mandel bread in large round tins from Florida to New York. It was decades ago, but the memory is still vivid of the joy Paul and his sister had in pulling off the tops of those tins; he can still conjure the aroma of that initial moment. Mandel bread in particular created some Jewish association between Paul and his grandmother because he understood—by not seeing that kind of cookie anywhere else—that this was something special being handed down from the distant past of his family. That recipe was unfortunately lost with her passing; sharing such baking "heirlooms" may serve as a bonding experience between mothers and daughters-in-law.

Send greeting cards when appropriate, and if possible include photos of yourself. Introduce your grandkids to tidbits of family history, anecdotes, connections to their past. Don't tell them the entire story at once, especially when they are young. Build the story over time so that it becomes their own.

Likewise, take an interest in your grandkids' activities. Some of this will, of course, come naturally, because you really do care. Still, it's important to remain cognizant of the ongoing conversation. The last thing you want to do is obsess over their Jewish activities (or lack thereof) at the expense of discussing what *they* love to do. If you haven't developed a full relationship with your grandchildren, the questions you ask or suggestions you offer about being Jewish might make you come off as a caricature.

Distance is a genuine challenge for any relationship, especially with children that grow and change so rapidly from one year to the next. But don't be afraid of it nor use distance as an excuse. And certainly don't wait for your grandchildren to initiate the contact. It may take some work on your part, and a lot of paying attention to seemingly disconnected stories, to follow all that is going on in your grandkids' lives between visits. But the payoff will be a stronger bond between you and your grandchildren, one that will have a positive impact throughout their lives.

14. PROVIDE FINANCIAL INCENTIVES.

Admittedly, paying the bills for your grandchildren to participate in activities and programs that will enhance their Jewish identity is a controversial suggestion. For some, financial situations will not make it possible to offer such incentives. But even for those who can afford it, or for the adult children who don't need the financial assistance of their parents, this is not about the money or their financial independence. Instead, this is about rewarding behaviors that are important to you—and communicating to your children and grandchildren about what is important. This is also about reducing any obstacles that may be impediments to participation. You can even establish an informal program that provides your grandchildren with the opportunity to "earn" their camp tuition or the fee for whatever activity you may be sponsoring.

It is not unusual, in general, for grandparents to pay for summer camp experiences, regardless of the specific camp the kids attend, nor for school tuition, for that matter. And we know that experiences such as Jewish summer camping are instrumental in nurturing Jewish identity and building Jewish peer groups. Thus it is important to take advantage of the resources available in the community to help you reach your goal of securing and fostering the Jewish identity of your grandchildren.

Obviously, the suggestion is controversial, because you don't want to appear to be "bribing" or, worse, "meddling." Offers of financial assistance can raise all sorts of issues about boundaries and appropriateness as your adult children establish their own families. And if this makes you uncomfortable, then we suggest that you don't consider it and skip this section. However, within the context of an ongoing, supportive dialogue it may feel like a natural extension of your relationship. Deciding to participate in Jewish activities ideally develops organically as a family, with your financial incentives serving as just that: added incentive. The goal is to "nudge" in the English definition of the word (give a gentle push) without becoming a *nudge* in the Yiddish definition (a pushy person).

Gladys told her adult children that she would be willing to give them the down payment on their new house or pay for its expansion or even the building of a swimming pool, if that's what they wanted, if they would allow her to pay the summer camp tuition for the grandchildren (for a mutually-agreed-upon camp).

You may feel that you can't afford such a large gesture or that it is too big a step to take. So start small. Be willing to pay for the annual dues of a junior or senior youth group or a youth membership to the local Jewish Community Center. Then take the offer one step further—and rest assured, your adult children will surely resonate with *this* offer—and volunteer to drive the grandkids back and forth to these events (if you are able to do so, and if you live in the same community). Sam told us that he simply arranged to pay for youth group member-ships for his grandchildren at a local synagogue as birthday presents (he made sure that that was not the only gift) and asked the synagogue to notify the kids that their memberships had been paid for by their grandfather. Who can turn down a birthday present from a grandparent?

As your grandchildren get older, invite them to participate in the selection process with you. Even if this process of pro-gram selection morphs somewhat into an initiative in youth philanthropy—that is, that you are together supporting a par-ticular organization or institution that means something to you and your grandchildren—you are enhancing their Jewish identity by emphasizing that such philanthropy is an activity whose foundation is based in Jewish values.

15. *F*IND JEWISH DESTINATIONS WHEN YOU TRAVEL, AND BRING YOUR GRANDCHILDREN WITH YOU.

Just about everyone loves to travel, especially if they aren't able to do so frequently. Visiting new places and sites of interest, including new restaurants and hotels, provides experiences that stay with us forever. You might not remember what you ate for breakfast this morning, but you'll never forget the crèpes they served on your hotel balcony in Paris twenty years ago. This is particularly the case with kids. Because travel experiences form such vivid memories, Jewish experiences when you travel enjoy an entirely different space in the minds of children. We encourage you to take your grandchildren traveling, with or without their parents—even if the travel is a short distance and doesn't include an overnight.

The Jewish people have lived in nearly every part of the world, so it's usually possible to tie the site you're visiting to something Jewish, whether you're in Chicago or China. Destinations that still contain vibrant Jewish communities provide the opportunity for you to demonstrate the connection you feel with global Jewry. Find out in advance what the Jewish community may have to offer, then be sensitive to the particular interests of your grandkids, so they can relate to the Jewish experience rather than be dragged through it.

75

For example, if your grandchild is interested in art, then see what kind of Jewish-related art and architecture may be available. Or if your grandchild studies music or dance, consider what opportunities may be available. But if your grandchildren are not interested in archaeology—even if you are—don't allow the tour guide to talk you into visiting "just one more site." This is particularly true for trips to Israel, where sites of archaeological interest abound and tour itineraries are overwhelmed by them. But there are plenty of exciting things for kids to do, too—like rafting down the Jordan River or taking off-road jeep tours in the north or hiking through the so-called "flour caves." And if they like archaeology, there are "digs for a day" that are interactive.

There are also times when kids like to take advantage of adult interests. They may like to get dressed up for a concert by a famous orchestra or an opera performance. Make sure that you give them that option, too. And in case they like a form of art or music that you don't like, let them lead the way.

Though it is harder to plan, making personal connections with local Jews can be a fascinating experience. This is as true in smaller North American cities as it is worldwide. Many a Jewish traveler has been drawn into Shabbat dinner with a mere mention of the connection. Comparing differences in customs can show the diversity of the Jewish people; of course, it helps when your grandkids are familiar with their own customs. Often such experiences lead children to want to incorporate some of what they have experienced into their own lives. What's important is the kinship felt between Jews that is often heightened when traveling, and that should be your focus. Let your grandkids experience firsthand that they are part of a larger worldwide community.

If it is possible, choose a time for your trip that may coincide with something special taking place in your destination city. For example, different Jewish holidays may be unique experiences in different cities. Some families take a vacation over Passover and do a communal *seder* in a Caribbean hotel. A number of large cities in the U.S. (such as New York and San Francisco) have large, fun events related to Israeli Independence Day. Thanks to the Chabad (Lubavitch) movement's outreach, there are large public menorah lightings in places as exotic as Red Square, Moscow. And there is a renaissance of Jewish life in many places in the former Soviet Union, so they can be part of the resurrection of Jewish communities by just traveling there and acquainting themselves with those communities.

It is also true that sometimes the most interesting travel destinations are right next door. If your grandkids live in a city of any notable size, odds are there's a site they haven't seen in their own town. That, too, may have a Jewish theme. And if you dig deeply together, you may discover a plethora of Jewish sites that are under the radar. But if your visit is a transparent attempt to get them to do something Jewish, you'll probably lose their interest before even arriving. If, however, the site is of genuine interest to all of you, and there's a Jewish element as well, it can be the kind of lifelong memory you're hoping to create.

Plan your trip carefully. Make arrangements ahead of time, but be flexible, so that plans can be changed if an interesting opportunity presents itself. In anticipation of the trip, keep the kids apprised. Send them brochures. Direct them to relevant websites. Send them on virtual tours. You may even want to send them a countdown calendar that you mark together—even at a distance. And make sure that the trip itself (getting there) is enjoyable.

Make sure to take lots of pictures. Get lots of meaningful souvenirs that will frequently rekindle the memories of the trip and will not simply be thrown away and forgotten once the child returns home. If possible, arrange for things to be mailed directly to your grandkids from the trip at designated intervals following your return home.

Even if your days end early at home, plan for a full day of activity each day while you are on the road. It is okay to schedule downtime, but be mindful of what kinds of downtime kids enjoy. Use the time to reflect on what you experienced and the building of your relationship through the sharing of memories.

16. STAY FOCUSED ON THE GOAL: RAISING THE LEVEL OF YOUR GRANDCHILDREN'S JEWISH ACTIVITY.

Be relentless in your pursuit. Don't worry what your friends say. And they may have lots to say. Much of it will be contrary to what you know is right and what you have to do. If they tell you to let *it* alone, that *it* isn't your business, that it is too late to do anything about the Jewish identity of your grand-children—even if they belittle you for your zeal—disregard comments from others. There are undoubtedly going to be distractions that threaten to throw you off course or dissuade you, since the task you have set for yourself may not be easy. Don't succumb to anything that has the potential to disarm you. Stay focused on the goal that you have set for yourself: Jewish activities and experiences with your grandkids.

Jewish memories are created by "doing Jewish." In this case, quantity is (for the most part) quality. The rule is simple: More is more. It is the only path to getting where we want to go—a positive Jewish identity for our grandchildren. All it takes is one such memory to jump-start a Jewish identity. The accumulation of these memories is what shapes and sustains Jewish identity, especially as these experiences and memories are carried into adulthood. They provide us with a foundation for who we are. Since memories are what Jewish education should be about, don't fret if your grandchild is not currently involved in formal Jewish education, as long as you are providing the context for accumulating such memories. An interest in formal education will come later—as late as taking Jewish Studies courses in college (which we have found to be a common under-exploited opportunity for the Jewish identity-building of the young adult children of the intermarried). This also means that your "activities" should not be reduced as the kids get older. Activities can change; they can ebb and flow over short periods of time, particularly during the rebellious years of adolescence, but they should not be curtailed.

Jewish household activity can take a variety of forms. Not all of it has to or should be related to ritual or holiday activity, even though those tend to be the easiest to access, especially for young children. And this is primarily what the community has to offer as well. But activities that involve the kitchen and food are usually a welcome place to begin. The environment is informal and friendly, and lots of information can be exchanged during the process of preparing family recipes or trying new ones together. The same is true if you are building something together in the garage, basement or back yard. Perhaps you may want to start with a *tzedakah* box or an oversized *menorah* for Hanukkah. We have an artist friend who built giant-sized spice boxes for *havdalah* out of wood. He believed—and we agree—that there is a lot of room for creative expression in ritual objects, way beyond what everyone says they are supposed to look like. Before we saw his unusual spice boxes, it hadn't occurred to us that spice boxes could be something larger than what would fit in one's hand.

Not all activities have to take place on a grand scale at first. Each subsequent activity you do with your grandchild is an increment and potentially an identity booster. If you have only limited opportunities for activities, choose wisely. Whatever you do, begin slowly so that you don't overwhelm the kids. This allows you to establish a foundation on which you can build. For it is on this foundation that your grandchild's Jewish identity can be forged. At the same time you will be nurturing your own identity, and your grandkids will see how important it is to you, too. So don't undertake these activities just for them; do them for yourself, too.

Jewish holidays are great informal learning tools because they repeat each year. While repetition may be a key to learning, your holiday celebrations should not feel *repetitious*. Yes, repeat the cherished rituals each year, including your own annual family traditions, but also throw in something new, if possible. The two most celebrated holidays, Hanukkah and Passover, allow for a lot of fun and flexibility. For example, bring blackjack chips and wear a dealer's visor to your next *dreidel* "tournament." Or have the kids act out the Passover plagues (or do it yourself!). Also, don't limit yourself to those two most-celebrated holidays. We've mentioned the costumed festival of Purim as a great introduction for celebrating in a synagogue, but what about building a *sukkah* on Sukkot? It's a big challenge that few Jews—even affiliated Jews—take on each year, but if a backyard is available, the attempt to build one will certainly become a lasting memory for everyone involved.

One of the things we have learned in our study of young adult children of intermarriage is that they see Jewish experiences in some secular cultural activities. For example, for most Americans, watching the film *Schindler's List* was a powerfully moving experience, but not a "Jewish" experience. For the children of intermarriage—even the least affiliated among them—it was a "Jewish" experience, as was watching *Fiddler on the Roof*. While these represent the most preliminary entry points into Jewish culture, they are entry points nonetheless, and, as we said above, more is better.

Since you have limited control over your grandchild's home environment and you probably do not want the activities with your grandchild in your home limited to Jewish ritual activities, it will be important to extend those activities beyond your home. Include them when you or your grandchildren are on the way somewhere, especially if you are involved in driving carpool or taking them to school. You can also leave activities unfinished that may require your grandchildren to do some things on their own at home, between visits with you—even simple art projects or basic research into a subject of mutual interest.

17. KEEP THE HOLIDAYS FOCUSED ON *CELEBRATION,* NOT CONFRONTATION.

People involved in intermarried families often speak of the so-called December dilemma. Anytime we speak with couples or make public presentations, the relationship between Hanukkah and Christmas eventually manifests itself in one way or another. Truthfully, we worry more when the issue of Hanukkah and Christmas does not surface. If an interfaith couple never talks about the December holidays, then it means they are probably not discussing the more difficult issues either, especially regarding children. On the other hand, if they are overly focused on this calendar issue without making room for anything else to enter into the discussion, that makes us worry, too.

Of course, December is not the only holiday period that contains potential conflicts. While their respective symbols do not seem as competitive with each other, the spring holidays of Easter and Passover often cause conflict in interfaith families, too, especially when relatives visit or when making decisions about which relatives to visit and when.

Overall, however, there is a large segment—perhaps the majority—of interfaith couples that have successfully navigated the issue to the point where it's no longer an issue...for them.

Their kids might understand it as "We celebrate Hanukkah at home, go to Daddy's parents' for Christmas dinner, and, oh, we have a Christmas tree for Daddy, but we're totally Jewish." We often like to say that these so-called holiday dilemmas are more of a dilemma for the Jewish community than they are for intermarried folks.

Members of the community find it unsettling, and you may as well, to see a Christmas tree in the home of their children. This is totally understandable. But don't write them off as a result of it. As hard—and perhaps painful—as it may be, if you visit during the holidays and your children have a Christmas tree, try not to focus your attention on it, because you are in a no-win situation. If you have always made clear your opposition to Jews having Christmas trees, your adult child will be braced for what you might say and already feel quite defensive, a potential tinderbox. If, on the other hand, you've never had an objection to the Christmas tree—and sometimes a tree is just a tree; many in-married Jewish immigrant families have put up trees because it was the "American" thing to do—if you were to suddenly begin objecting now because of the context of the intermarriage, you would only seem hypocritical.

While we would all prefer that the tree not be in any home in which Jews live, especially when we are trying to influence the Jewish identity of grandchildren, there is no reason to believe that the presence of a Christmas tree alone will negatively impact the developing Jewish identity of your grandchild. The same thing is true about participation in events related to Easter, such as an Easter egg hunt, or other holiday activities. Many of these activities will disappear as your grandchildren grow older in any case, especially since they are often being observed without any religious connection.

But here's what we consider to be the really difficult challenge: staying away from things that lie under the surface of your relationship with your children and grandchildren that emerge during the holiday period even if they are not directly related to it. This is particularly difficult when you don't live close to your children and your visits understandably coincide with holiday seasons. As a result, while some important things may get discussed over the telephone or through e-mail, it is more common to discuss things of importance face-to-face. Moreover, you may not even realize that certain things have to be discussed until you have encountered something in your children's home.

For example, some parents don't make decisions about their children until they are forced to do so or until specific events require it. As a rule, it is generally better to make important decisions when you have the benefit of time and are not forced to make them quickly. Nevertheless, perhaps your adult children still have not made a decision regarding the religious upbringing or education of your grandchild. The presence of an Easter basket may cause you to draw the conclusion that a decision has been made in favor of the Christian religion, or it may remind you yet again that no decision has yet been made. So you choose (unwisely, we caution) to raise the issue about the religious upbringing of your grandchildren, which you prefer to be in the Jewish religion. As a result, what you may see as an educational issue quickly becomes associated with the holiday season, especially if your opportunity to interact with your children is limited to such periods of time. Your visits—since such discussion inevitably will cause friction—become less welcome to your children and perhaps even your grandchildren, if they hear the interaction or they see how your relationship with your children—their parents—has changed.

We recommend leaving the actual conversation for a later time, so as not to dampen the holidays or create negative associations with your visits. And as we've suggested throughout this book, you may need to lead by example rather than nagging from the sidelines. Instead of "When are you going to decide about..." try "I'd like to offer my help (either in a time commitment or financially) in getting little Jimmy into a Jewish preschool," for example. Always ask yourself if you are making positive gestures of support rather than negative criticisms.

Often such a discussion also brings up "stuff" (that's the technical term!) that remains unresolved from the decisions about religious education and even religious observance you made with regard to your own children when they were young. Since our own Jewish identity constantly evolves, it is possible that you are in a different place today with regard to Jewish observance than you were when your own children were young. So you want your children to benefit from your experience. And that's where the disconnect appears. Holiday memories (or those that your children are trying to create for your grandchildren) may be what bring up the issues for them as well.

Don't let us kid you. It will not be simple or easy to stay focused on your visit and not on all the other issues that you want to discuss. It will take discipline and inner strength to do what needs to be done and, at the same time, avoid undoing what has already been done. Just stay the course.

18. *D*ON'T CONFUSE SUPPORT FOR YOUR INTERMARRIED FAMILY MEMBERS WITH SUPPORT FOR INTERMARRIAGE ITSELF.

If you are an active member of the organized Jewish community, maybe even one of its leaders, you are well aware of the posture of many within the community toward intermarriage and the intermarried. The attitude of the community may be generally characterized at best as tolerance. In many places it is better described as downright disdain. While it may not be true of the majority of individuals in the Jewish community, it is particularly true of what we call "core community institutions." This attitude is surely one reason that so many intermarried families stay away from these institutions. You may project some of these less-than positive-attitudes without realizing it, even as you are trying hard to find a way to relate to your adult child who is married to someone who is not Jewish and to their children, your grandchildren. Perhaps you may simply feel ambivalent about the partner choice that your child has made as you try to navigate between the dreams and desires you had for your children (especially when they were younger) and the decisions they have made as adults.

It is indeed difficult to support the "ideal" of in-marriage while at the same time supporting your children and the decisions that they have made, as well as trying to develop a relationship with your grandchildren and nurture their Jewish identity. But it is not impossible. To be sure, it is not a simple process. Moreover, it is not a decision that gets made once so you can be done with it. Instead it is a decision and approach that has to be revisited many times over the course of a lifetime. There is one thing to keep in mind, however—perhaps the most important thing, irrespective of these general attitudes. These kids are your grandchildren. No communal policy or attitude can change that. And just as communities will not make general decisions while thinking how such decisions will affect your grandchildren, you (and your children) do not make decisions about your grandchildren while thinking how those decisions will impact the community or the Jewish people in general.

That is why it is so important that you separate the attitude of the community from the attitude you express to members of your family. Actually, we hope that it works the other way around: that fostering a relationship with your grandchildren will color your approach to the community, especially when it comes to challenging its many exclusionary policies and practices. When the Jewish community chooses to assume such an exclusionary posture, it is closing its doors to many hundreds of thousands of people, including your children and grandchildren.

While some people will want to equate your approach to your grandchildren—as children of intermarried parents—with support for intermarriage itself, don't let them do so. They may even try to make the false claim that such an approach actually *encourages* and fosters intermarriage. Nothing could be further from the truth. It is like saying that teaching safe sex to teenagers promotes sexual promiscuity among them. One thing has nothing to do with the other. Responsible parents and educators teach safe sex even as they teach reasoned decision-making. They hope that children do not engage in sexual activity until they are ready to do so. Yet, they also realize that they have a responsibility to their children to prepare them for the world, recognizing that some will engage in sexual activity earlier than others. Similarly, even if you were to point out the challenges of interfaith marriages to young adults prior to their developing a relationship with a non-Jewish person, such relationships are usually not planned. Interfaith relationships generally just happen. They result from attending universities and from being in secular work environments and general social contexts. It is an interaction with North American society and a liberal social ethic that provides the environmental mix for interfaith marriages to emerge. No one thing actually promotes it. And there is no reason to believe that any specific attitudes discourage it, either. What such attitudes will encourage is a desire among interfaith families to disassociate themselves from a judgmental community or family. Even the issue of interdating, which once was understood as the primary precursor to interfaith marriage, has changed. Now that people go out more with groups of friends than on traditional dates as they once did, the place of interdating in the so-called interfaith marriage continuum has changed as well.

You have an opportunity to change the attitude of your community toward interfaith marriage as a direct result of your child's interfaith marriage and the fate of your grandchil-

91

dren. In-marriage is important because it represents a primary vehicle for perpetuating Jewish life and values. But it is not the only vehicle, nor can the perpetuation of Judaism take place by in-marriage alone. You may not have wanted to be a spokesperson for a cause, particularly such a delicate and difficult one, but you may be destined to be one in any case. By being an advocate for your grandchildren in the community, and for their parents, your grandchildren will see once again how important their Jewish identity and their ability to participate in the Jewish community is to you. While trying to find their own place in the community as they grow older, they will also see that the value of inclusiveness is a core value in Judaism.

For people who use arguments against "intermarriage" to exclude "the intermarried" from participation in the Jewish community, you must have a clear response. And in understanding your response, you may even change your own attitudes. We have a simple catchphrase at JOI (Jewish Outreach Institute) that we believe speaks volumes, and it's become one of our mantras: "Intermarriage does not end Jewish continuity; not raising Jewish children ends Jewish continuity."

Think about it. Every single Jewish person in America (outside the insular ultra-Orthodox community) can name at least one intermarried couple raising Jewish children and creating a strongly identified Jewish household. JOI calls them "Successful Jewish Intermarriages" and believes the community should be holding up these households as models. Yes, the statistics tell us those families are in the minority of intermarried households...RIGHT NOW. But the fact that we all know such families proves that it can be done, and our goal is to get more such families to do it. And your goal is to get one such family—that of your intermarried adult child—to do it. So it is time for all of us to lose the blanket statements about intermarriage and instead start focusing on the raising of Jewish children by *all* Jewish households, whether they are in-married or intermarried. And when it happens, we must praise those families, be they in-married or intermarried. And when it doesn't happen, we must continue to make our assistance available in the hope that it will, regardless of whether they are in-married or inter-married.

19. DON'T GO IT ALONE; IT TAKES A COMMUNITY TO RAISE JEWISH GRANDCHILDREN.

Whether as a single parent or with a fulltime partner, you probably raised your children by yourself—that is, no one else did it for you. Of course, you had some help along the way, whether that help took the form of only an occasional babysitter or even a full-time childcare provider. Like most people, the help you received was probably somewhere between full-time and part-time. It probably changed as your needs and those of your children changed. Perhaps your own parents helped along the way, maybe more so when the children were younger. And don't forget other relatives and friends and pediatricians and teachers and all of the other people that play important roles in the life of a child. As independent as we often think we are, there are few things—especially things as important as raising children—that we can actually do by ourselves. In fact, there are often others who spend even more time with our children than we do.

As a grandparent, you may now be in the important support role in which others served when you first became a parent. If you live with your grandchildren or in such close proximity that you see them quite frequently, you may actually spend as much time with them as anyone else, and that will obviously afford you a tremendous opportunity to influence their lives. Even if you live far away, however, it's important to think about all of the people who can positively influence your grandchildren beyond simply their parents. The bottom line: Don't try to nurture the Jewish identity of your grandchildren on your own. Get others to help you.

Unfortunately, it may be more difficult than it should be to enlist the resources of the Jewish community, especially if you were never part of it or have separated yourself from it. If you live in a rural or small community, there may be fewer Jewish institutions, and therefore a greater effort is required on your part. But as our friend Macy Hart of the Institute of Southern Jewish Life likes to remind us, his parents drove him 90 minutes every Sunday morning when he was a child to make sure he was able to attend Sunday school—that was the synagogue closest to his home. People make the extra effort to do things that are important to them, and securing the Jewish identity of your grandchild is certainly of utmost importance.

You may want to use the occasion of rising to the challenge of nurturing your grandchildren's Jewish identity to reconnect with the local Jewish community or even participate in it for the first time, if you have never really been involved. To connect might necessitate becoming a dues-paying member of a synagogue or Jewish Community Center. You will quickly find that you are not alone in this enterprise. There are literally thousands of other grandparents facing the same challenges and obstacles and frustrations that you now face. Get to know them. Share your strategies with them. Don't be afraid—or embarrassed—to open up to them. You will find hidden strengths in one another. Together you can discover what resources your community has to offer and how they can benefit you and be shared with your grandchildren.

If your local Jewish community doesn't provide you with all the services you think you need, make sure that you communicate your needs to leaders of the community. Often community leaders don't know what kinds of services people need simply because people don't tell them. Unfortunately, too often these leaders haven't bothered to ask. There are also national Jewish community resources that local community organizations and institutions can help you access. (The Jewish Outreach Institute is one such organization, providing programs and resources nationally and in local communities.)

We usually do not have the opportunity to make the same choices with regard to who will impact the lives of our grandchildren as we once did with our own children. In some cases we can make suggestions to adult children about the choices they intend to make for their children, but we can only offer suggestions. (This means that we can't get upset when they choose not to follow our suggestions, nor can we say "I told you so" when the decision they made that were contrary to the suggestions we offered don't work out.) That is why we have to enlist the support of others in our quest to secure the Jewish identity of our grandchildren. Often others can be persuasive in areas where we can't be.

Be creative in thinking about the resources available to help with your grandchildren, how to identify them and where to find them, because the landscape will vary from community to community. As with everything else, this is more challeng-

97

ing to do from longer distances, but either way it may take some serious networking in person or over the phone. What you're looking for is that one Jewish community professional (or volunteer) who can serve as your guide. This person will actually listen to you, understand your family's situation, and provide a variety of options for Jewish events and programs of interest. Creating more of these welcoming guides into the Jewish community is a part of JOI's work, because there are certainly not enough of them. But there are some such folks out there, and once you find them, you'll be glad you spent a little time hunting them down.

Take, for example, Rosanne Levitt of San Francisco, who founded the Interfaith Connection program (and although now retired has left her legacy in the capable hands of Helena McMahon), or Dawn Kepler across the bridge in the East Bay. If your adult children lived in the Bay Area, you could get in touch (or put them in touch) with one of these experienced Jewish professionals, who do amazing work with what you might call "persistent kindness." Rosanne has told us about families who have lingered on her database for years without participating in any programs, but whom Rosanne would still call periodically, just to check in and let them know that the Jewish community was there for them whenever they were ready. The overwhelming response from the families she contacted was appreciation for the reminder, and many did indeed—finally—take her up on her offer when the time was right for them or, more likely, for their young children. Coming from you, your adult children may find constant reminders to be annoying nudging or interference. Coming from a kind yet "impartial" stranger like Rosanne, it felt like a warm welcome into a community that otherwise might have been difficult to navigate.

Such trained professionals will understand how to lower barriers to participation in Jewish life for your unaffiliated children and grandchildren. They will find programs that require no prior Jewish knowledge; that don't cost a lot (or anything) to participate in; that center on fun family holidays; and that don't require heavy time commitments. Lowering these and other barriers leads to programs that will be more appealing to families who feel cautious about engaging the Jewish community. Gradually, as they become more familiar with the community, they will feel more comfortable making a deeper engagement. But to start, let's offer those fun, welcoming, entry-level programs before we start asking for a deeper commitment. Finding the supportive Jewish professional to guide you toward those programs is a good way to begin.

20. *I*T CAN WORK. IT DOES WORK.

This book has tried to express one important message throughout that can best be summarized in this phrase: Sustained hard work can and does make a difference. You probably already know that from your life experiences. If we work at it tirelessly, we can nurture the nascent Jewish identity of our interfaith grandchildren. And our research indicates that these children do carry with them a spark of Jewish identity, no matter how dimly illuminated that spark may seem. But in the case of your grandchildren, we want you to take this notion that it can work as your daily *kavannah*, a sacred mantra, the one that you repeat to yourself each morning. Repeat it over and over to yourself, especially when you feel that things seem out of your control (and much of life is indeed out of our control), when they don't seem to be going the way you want, the way you have planned. It is this optimism that comes from our work with interfaith families that we have tried to share with you in these pages and that will help you to move forward.

Sometimes the entirety of one's effort can be summed up in one or two sentences. That is what we feel when grandparents have told us, as they often do, that the methods work. "You know, you are right," one grandparent recently said, "I didn't think that I could do it. I didn't think that it could work. I found out that my granddaughter signed up for a trip to Israel. I didn't know that she wanted to go. Had she told me, I would have even paid for it. But I am just so thrilled."

We know that we can make a rational case for how to grandparent your interfaith grandchild. We can advise you on particular methods and approaches, as we do regularly in our daily work with interfaith families. What we can't do is persuade your heart to hear what you already know in your head. We leave that task up to you. So shut out the noise of others who may be trying to persuade you to do something different. Just know that the more your work at it, the more your heart will believe what your head is saying.

Think of yourself as an advocate now, because consciously or not, you are advocating on a number of fronts. You are advocating on behalf of Judaism to your children and grandchildren by sharing what you love about it, by providing guidance and encouragement, and by modeling through your own life and actions. You are advocating on behalf of your children and grandchildren to your peers in the Jewish community, if you are actively involved, by demanding a place at the table for your intermarried family members. In some ways you may be advocating on behalf of your grandchildren to your own children that they be given the exposure to Jewish culture and community. However you may find yourself advocating, do what a good advocate does. Prepare your message, stick to that message, and live that message beyond reproach. Even those who will not agree with what we advocate will nevertheless admire our steadfastness so long as our message is based on rational thinking rather than anger or stubbornness.

We hope the prior chapters have helped you prepare your "messages" and tailor them to your various "audiences." But you will have to write the actual script yourself, because every family is unique and every situation different. As your grandchildren grow older your relationship with them will change, just as it continues to change with their parents, your own children. On some days, especially during their adolescence, you may feel you are having little impact on them. This is normal. During adolescence children listen to their peers much more than anyone else. At this time in their lives you may have more in common with their parents than at any other time during their lives. You may all feel "you don't have a clue," and in case you are wondering, your grandchildren will regularly remind you. And if they don't tell you, then their actions will certainly do the necessary communication. In reality, grandparents sometimes have a greater opportunity to impact grandchildren during their adolescence—when they are rejecting their own parents—than do the parents. So take advantage of this opportunity. This book is, therefore, not just for grandparents with young grandchildren; it is also for the grandparents of adolescent grandchildren.

The days will surely be inconsistent. Sometimes you will feel you are having a greater impact on your grandchildren than on other days. If you are a long-distance grandparent, the feeling may be exacerbated, as the opportunities you have to affect your grandchildren are generally less frequent when you live far from them and don't see them regularly.

If you will excuse the analogy, what we are suggesting is similar to making a financial investment to secure your future, maybe even your retirement. If you watch a specific stock on a daily basis and consider its ups and downs, you may make yourself crazy. But if you step back and analyze your performance over a greater period of time, you may see a wholly different financial picture. It is always important to step back, to celebrate small victories, and to consider the entire picture. Small steps forward advance us just as surely as do quantum leaps. As much as we might like to see quantum leaps forward, just as we wish our financial portfolios would make large gains in short periods of time, this is infrequently the case. To cast this approach in more religious terms, perhaps we need to focus on the small miracles of daily living rather than the world-changing miracles out of which the Torah is made. And small steps, like small miracles, are much more realistic when we are attempting to mold young souls and their Jewish identities.

We have a lot riding on the nurturing work you are doing with your grandchildren. That is why we want to make sure it works. Just as the Rabbis said that when God gave the Jewish people the Torah they put up the *children* of Israel as guarantors for the future of the ancient Jewish people, your grandchildren remain as the guarantors of the future of the modern Jewish people. And just as your Judaism didn't necessarily reflect the Judaism of your parents and grandparents, neither will the Judaism of your grandchildren. It is already vastly different simply because of the world in which we live. Nonetheless, your future, our future, the future of the entire Jewish community depends on them—and on you. That is why your continuous effort is so important. To characterize the task you are embarking on by paraphrasing the text of the Rabbis of *Pirke*

Avot, one of the most quoted books in the so-called oral Torah, we can say it simply this way: "You are not required to do all the work, but you aren't allowed to shirk your responsibility either."

We recognize that it will not be an easy task. In our experience, little that is worthwhile is easy. But the rewards can be immeasurable. All of your effort, no matter how many challenges you encounter along the way, will be worth it.

Obviously, there are no guarantees. But if you don't try, you will have plenty of regrets and few to blame but yourself.

When you have moments of doubt, and there will surely be plenty of them, remember that you are not working alone. A growing number of members in the Jewish community understand the importance of outreach to intermarried families and their children. We are here to help.

And also remember that others are doing the same thing as you are doing—and doing it successfully.

As our friend Michael Rukin likes to say, it is time to stop asking, "How Jewish is the contemporary American Jewish community?" (In this case, "How Jewish are your grandchildren?") Rather, we should be focusing on the question: *How are they Jewish?* And in so doing, you will see the progress that you make, slow and tedious as it may sometimes seem.

The progress you seek regarding your grandchildren's Jewish identity may not happen all at once—and we recognize that it doesn't happen for everyone—but continue to work at it. Our world depends on it.

RABBI KERRY M. OLITZKY is the executive director of the Jewish Outreach Institute (JOI) in New York, the only national organization that provides programs and services for interfaith families, advocating for a more inclusive Jewish community. He is well-known for his many inspirational books that bring the wisdom of Jewish tradition into everyday life, including many books on Jewish spirituality, healing, and religious practice.

PAUL GOLIN is assistant executive director of JOI and author of the report "The Coming Majority: Suggested Action on Intermarried Households for the Organized Jewish Community."

Other helpful titles:

Creating a Successful Jewish Interfaith Marriage: The Jewish Outreach Institute Guide to Challenges, Opportunities and Resources by Rabbi Kerry M. Olitzky with Joan Peterson Littman. Jewish Lights Publishing.

Introducing My Faith and Community: The Jewish Outreach Institute Guide for the Christian in a Jewish Interfaith Relationship by Rabbi Kerry M. Olitzky. Jewish Lights Publishing.

Jewish Holidays: A Brief Introduction for Christians by Rabbi Kerry M. Olitzky and Rabbi Dan Judson. Jewish Lights Publishing.

Jewish Ritual: A Brief Introduction for Christians by Rabbi Kerry M. Olitzky and Rabbi Dan Judson. Jewish Lights Publishing.